"In a serious world filled with trials and uncertainty, when was the last time someone challenged you to discover genuine *joy*? Though joy may seem like a luxury we can't afford, Tommy Newberry reminds us that life was meant to be lived with energy, fulfillment, purpose—and yes, *joy*. I have personally watched Tommy teach some of the top business people in the country how to adopt his 4:8 Principle mind-set in their workplaces *and* families. The tangible, positive results they've experienced have been tremendous. His teaching and mentoring—now available to you and me in book form—can make a world of difference in how we approach life today and where our lives, families, and contributions to others' lives can end up tomorrow."

JOHN TRENT, PH.D., president, The Center for StrongFamilies

"Get ready to transform your mind! With a no-nonsense approach, Tommy Newberry will nudge you out of your comfort zone and revolutionize your thinking. He'll also show you the way to experience joy in your life like you never have before."

LES PARROTT, PH.D., founder of RealRelationships.com and author of 3 Seconds

"With *The 4:8 Principle,* Tommy Newberry has again established himself as the premier authority on achieving and enjoying true success in life. You can become everything God created you to become when you reprogram your mind with the timeless principles and practical message clearly described in this book. I have used and shared Tommy's teachings for years, and after reading *The 4:8 Principle,* I was amazed at both its simplicity and its power to make our lives lives of joy. You'll want to read this over and over again!"

BILL ORENDER, senior national sales director, Primerica Financial Services

"In *The 4:8 Principle*, Tommy Newberry has taken the apostle Paul's prescription for living a joy-filled life and made it available and practical for everyone. With wisdom and insight, Tommy gives real-life examples and clear advice for changing your focus, transforming negatives into positives, and more important, how to share this powerful principle with others."

DON AND CHERYL BARBER, hosts of the award-winning TV program *goodnews don&cheryl*

"As a clinical psychologist, I frequently see how negative and self-destructive patterns of thinking not only lead to a variety of personal and relational problems but also severely limit our full potential. In *The 4:8 Principle*, Tommy Newberry clearly and effectively shows us how to transform old, negative patterns of thinking into new, productive ones, using solid biblical truths. The wisdom in this book can be applied by anyone—starting today! I will use these powerful, life-changing tools in my own life and in my clinical practice."

MARK E. CRAWFORD, PH.D., clinical psychologist and author of *When Two Become Three: Nurturing Your Marriage After Baby Arrives*

"With fist-pounding passion and clarity, Tommy Newberry nails the truth in *The 4:8 Principle*. I urge you to listen up. A new way of life is possible."

NORM EVANS, president of Pro Athletes Outreach and former NFL All-Pro

THE SECRET TO A JOY-FILLED LIFE

TOMMY
NEWBERRY

THE 4:8 PRINCIPLE

TYNDALE HOUSE PUBLISHERS, INC.

CAROL STREAM, ILLINOIS

Visit Tyndale's exciting Web site at www.tyndale.com

Library of Congress Cataloging-in-Publication Data

Newberry, Tommy.
  The 4:8 principle : the secret to a joy-filled life / Tommy Newberry.
    p. cm.
  ISBN-13: 978-1-4143-1304-7 (hc)
  ISBN-10: 1-4143-1304-7 (hc)
  1. Joy—Religious aspects—Christianity. 2. Thought and thinking—Religious aspects—Christianity. I. Title.
  BV4647.J68N49 2007
  248.4—dc22   2007010405

Printed in the United States of America

13 12 11 10 09 08 07
 7   6   5   4   3

*This book is joyfully dedicated to my wife, Kristin,
and my three sons, Ty, Mason, and Brooks*

By Tommy Newberry

BOOKS

The 4:8 Principle

Success Is Not an Accident

366 Days of Wisdom & Inspiration

AUDIO

Success Is Not an Accident: Secrets of the Top 1%

Order your copy at www.tommynewberry.com

CP0114

CONTENTS

ACKNOWLEDGMENTS

Though it is virtually impossible for me to list all the people who have influenced me and contributed to *The 4:8 Principle,* I do want to recognize a special few who helped make this book a reality. Special thanks to my agent, Pamela Harty, who believed in me and in this particular project and helped make it happen. Thanks to Carol Traver at Tyndale House Publishers who caught the vision for this book, saw its importance, and supplied the deadlines that compelled me to write. Thank you to Karin Buursma, and Dave Lindstedt from Tyndale, who meticulously examined every word in the manuscript and challenged me to clarify, simplify, and illustrate the key points in the most effective way possible. Readers will greatly benefit because of your experience, insight, and attention to detail.

Thanks to my good friend and business partner, Steve Cesari, whose ideas and feedback both directly and indirectly sharpened many of the concepts in this book. Thank you to The 1% Club's assistant coaches—Jan West, Michele Zakeri, and Sara Bouman—whose creativity and tactical support allowed this project to be completed in the midst of many other pressing demands.

Thanks to my parents, who as far as my memory serves me, affirmed me repeatedly in 4:8 fashion with the phrase "We're very proud of you," even when uttering those words probably required quite a leap of faith. I am grateful for my grandmother Lillian Mason, who first explained to me as a child the importance of a positive attitude in dealing with both the successes and setbacks of life. I want to thank my wife, Kristin, who encourages me continually and intuitively practices the 4:8 Principle as a wife, mom, and friend. I love you!

Most of all, I want to thank God for giving me the desire, the patience, the wise counsel, and especially this specific opportunity to impact the world with *The 4:8 Principle: The Secret to a Joy-Filled Life.*

THINKING LIKE GOD THINKS

All things be ready if our minds be so.
– William Shakespeare

This is not a book about thinking like most people think. You do not need a book for that; it just happens naturally! *The 4:8 Principle* is a book about thinking differently, about thinking in a way that maximizes your *potential for joy*. Because most people are oblivious to their habitual way of thinking, they experience less joy and a less-abundant life than God intended for them.

I wrote this book to help you improve the one thing in life over which you have complete control: your thinking. This profoundly influences every other aspect of your life. In my practice as a life coach, I've observed that all lasting change is preceded by changed thinking. Any other type of change will be only temporary. The place to begin, then, is with your thought life, with a revival of your mind. I have great news for you: You no longer have to be a slave to your thoughts!

Few people have experience with intentional, focused thinking. We spend very little time thinking about what we are thinking about. For most of us, thinking is a poorly developed ability that often occurs with little conscious awareness. You can probably go through hours—even days and weeks—filled with frenzied activity while giving very little notice to the *quality of thoughts* passing through your mind. Most of your thinking is more like background noise while you engage in other activities. Yet behind everything you do is a thought, and each individual thought contributes to your overall character. How well your mind works dictates how much joy you experience, how successful you feel, and how well you interact with other people. **No area of your life is untouched by your thoughts.** Your habitual thinking patterns either encourage you toward excellence or nudge you into weakness.

By the grace of God, each moment is a new beginning, a new dawn for your potential. Your thoughts can become totally different, and as a result, your character can change and your life can be transformed. God wants you to be completely alive, full of passion, and bursting with joy. After all, we're his children—and would you want anything less for your children? King David vividly illustrated God's desire when he wrote these words to the Lord: "You turned my wailing into dancing; you removed my sackcloth and clothed me with joy" (Psalm 30:11, NIV). God desires us to experience great joy, and he created us with that capacity. He wants good things for us and has a wonderful plan for our future!

You can become everything God had in mind when he created you. There is no limit to your full potential once you recognize and put into practice the secret to a joy-filled life. Despite your past and regardless of your current circumstances, your future can exceed even your wildest expectations. There is only one catch: *You must learn to think like God thinks!*

You may be wondering, *How could I possibly do that?* Well, of course it's impossible to literally think like God—he is all-knowing and all-powerful. But we can learn to focus our thoughts on things that reflect and honor his character. It's not easy, but it is simpler than you might realize—and it will pay great dividends. The truly difficult thing is living with the consequences of *not* changing the way you think. As with many other defining moments in life, you have the choice to pay now or pay later. If you choose to postpone payment by not changing your thinking, the later cost, with compounded interest, will always be even greater.

How Does God Think?

To understand how God thinks, we must first comprehend *who* God is. With just a quick glimpse through the Bible, we learn that

- God is love.
- God is all-powerful.
- God is ever present.
- God is all knowing.
- God is absolute truth.
- God is holy.
- God is merciful.
- God is faithful.
- God is just.
- God is unchanging.

Though not exhaustive, this description of God's nature certainly gives us enough clues to contemplate the perfection and unlimited character of our Creator. To think like God, you must become intentional about mirroring his image in all that you do. Nowhere is this more important than in your thought life. As your thoughts reflect God's thoughts, not only will you glorify God, but you will also increase your positive influence on those you love. No doubt you will become a much brighter light to many whom you may never meet personally. God wants to impart his character and power through every individual. And when this happens, the world is instantly changed because those who reflect his glory impact the world.

The Scripture verse on which this book is based is Philippians 4:8, written by the apostle Paul:

> Finally, brethren, whatever things are true, whatever things are noble, whatever things are just, whatever things are pure, whatever things are lovely, whatever things are of good report, if there is any virtue and if there is anything praiseworthy—meditate on these things. (NKJV)

If anyone was ever justified in being negative and overwhelmed, certainly Paul was. Unfairly accused, confined in prison, and facing death, he chose to emphasize possibilities instead of problems. In his letters, he challenged believers to think differently and rise above the world's standard. As a prisoner, he didn't whine about the poor conditions, his bad luck, being chained to the guards, or even the things he missed about being free. Instead, Paul wrote in a spirit of gratitude and with an encouraging, joyful manner—all in the midst of a continual barrage of persecution. The apostle Paul presents us with exceedingly wise advice for thinking like God thinks when he challenges us to seek out and dwell on the positives in our life.

Philippians 4:8 reflects very crisply the nature and character of God, who himself is true, noble, just, pure, lovely, and of good report. As Christians, we are called to meditate on things that mirror God's character! Not only does this keep us from focusing on sinful or harmful things, but it also allows us to fill our lives with hope and optimism.

From time to time, you might hear a sermon preached on this passage, encouraging people to focus their minds on positive, beneficial things. Most people who hear this message nod their heads and agree with it in theory. However, what really counts is putting the 4:8 Principle *into practice,* and that's where this book comes in.

Joy by Design!

In *The 4:8 Principle,* I will challenge some of your dearest assumptions and possibly nudge you out of your comfort zone. But I promise that it will be well worth the effort. Since 1991, I have worked as a life coach for more than eight hundred highly successful clients in The 1% Club, and many thousands more in my public speaking events. I have used the principles you're about to learn to help people just like you revitalize their minds, get unstuck from disagreeable conditions, and go on to leave their unique mark on the world. In the chapters that follow, I'll show you how you might be snuffing out some of the light that God intended to shine through your life. Then I will show you step-by-step how to think more like God and upgrade your potential for joy. When you live in alignment with the 4:8 Principle, you beget a series of positive life changes in you and those you love for generations to come.

In the pages that follow, I'll challenge you to *discover, develop,* and *defend* your joy. In each of these sections, you will find field-tested strategies, sensible suggestions, and sustainable approaches to living a joy-filled life. Beginning today, you'll learn how to

- Create a fresh start
- Upgrade your "joy software"
- Eliminate destructive emotions
- Develop immunity to negative influences
- Express exceptional gratitude.

I wrote *The 4:8 Principle* to propel you into new ways of thinking, speaking, and acting. For the remainder of this book, think of me as your coach. My goal is to help you achieve your goals! Whether you are at a low point or a high point in your life, this book can help you get to the next level and beyond. It is joy by design—*God's design*.

Are you ready to be full of joy? This is the time. Today is the day. Let's get started!

Finally, brethren,

whatever things are true,

whatever things are noble,

whatever things are just,

whatever things are pure,

whatever things are lovely,

whatever things are of good report,

if there is any virtue and

if there is anything praiseworthy—

meditate on these things.

PHILIPPIANS 4:8 (NKJV)

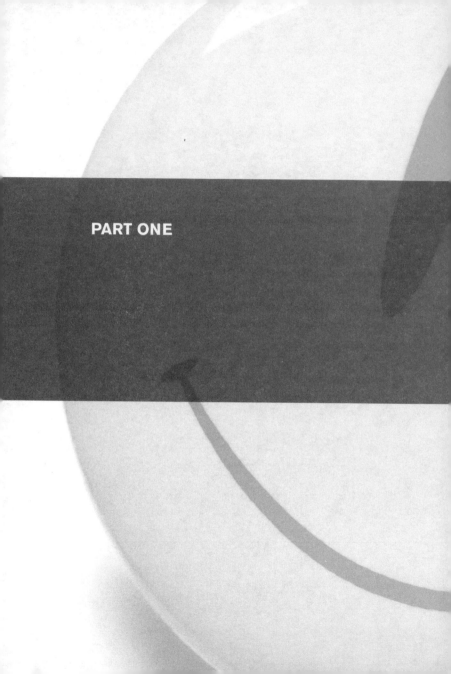

PART ONE

THINK ON THESE THINGS

Discovering Your Joy

CHAPTER 1

LIFE AS IT WAS MEANT TO BE

Discovering the Secret to a Joy-Filled Life

If you only care enough for a result, you will almost certainly attain it. Only you must then really wish these things, and wish them exclusively, and not wish at the same time a hundred other incompatible things just as strongly.

– William James

What is the secret to a joy-filled life? Does such a thing even exist? Since the beginning of time, mankind has searched just about everywhere in hopes of finding out this secret. Today, most people are trying to find joy in something or someone outside of themselves. But where exactly did God place this secret to a joy-filled life? Is it possible that our heavenly Father branded joy onto the very fiber of our being? I think God gave all of us a shot at experiencing the proactive happiness I call joy. After all, we are his most beloved creation.

As humans, we search for joy in all the wrong places. And what we receive is just a sporadic sampling, a fraction of the real deal, a clever counterfeit to genuine joy. We look outside, not inside. The secret to a joy-filled life is so close, so obvious, that inside is often the last place we look. We search everywhere but within.

Living with joy is our birthright. It is God's intention for all his children. In 1 Thessalonians, the apostle Paul writes,

"Be joyful always; pray continually; give thanks in all circumstances, for this is God's will for you in Christ Jesus" (5:16-18, NIV). As children of God, we are rightful heirs to the blessing of overflowing joy. God has declared us worthy. As a result, we have a calling, a responsibility to express and demonstrate joy by the way we live.

Being joy filled does not mean that your life is perfect. Who could claim that? It doesn't even mean that your life is great. What it does mean is that you emphatically trust God and believe that he has great plans for your life, regardless of what is happening right now. Joy is the infectious and uncontainable fruit of divinely inspired growth. It's a deeply entrenched, unshakable belief, the result of sustained right thinking and dwelling on the nature and character of God. **Joy is an outward sign of inward faith in the promises of God.** It is a way of acting, and it is evidence of spiritual maturity. Joy is not a distant destination at which you arrive; rather, it's a path you choose to travel each day.

Joy is the sum and substance of emotional health. It is a state of mind that must be deliberately cultivated if you are determined to live and love and influence others as God intended. How do you cultivate joy? To begin with, you make the decision never again to settle for anything less than real joy. Independent of outer conditions, joy is the result of practicing what I call the 4:8 Principle. We'll talk about that more in the next chapter.

My two oldest boys have figured out that I am not the most complex guy in the world. When we're playing capture the flag with their friends, I often hide the flag out in the open, almost in plain view. You guessed it—for a long time it's the last place any of the kids look. When playing hide-and-seek, I'll often hide in the same spot two or three times in a row, consistently escaping detection (at least for a little while). Our human nature, with an assist from modern culture, promotes the idea that solutions must be deep and complicated to be valuable. In most cases, nothing could be further from the truth. Lasting solutions are surprisingly simple. **Joy is within us, but it must be released.**

Keep Your Thoughts Fixed on God!

Mental discipline is the ability to keep your thoughts consistently focused. When you use the 4:8 Principle as the filter for your thinking, you focus on God and goodness to the exclusion of all else. As a result, you will begin to develop mental strength. With high levels of mental discipline, you'll reach your goals faster, upgrade your potential for joy, and become a lot more fun to be around. When you keep your thoughts fixed on God, the things of God will naturally permeate your life, and thus your goals will be in line with his will and his kingdom. Virtually any meaningful goal is within reach when you become mentally disciplined. Without the positive focus demanded by the 4:8 Principle, even relatively easy goals become a strain to reach.

With weak mental muscles, the existence of joy in your life is random and unpredictable. Mental laziness slowly dissolves your potential for joy—first privately, in your thoughts, and then publicly, coming out in your actions and circumstances. The concept of mental discipline may sound scary or even intimidating, but a life without mental discipline is far more daunting. It may be a challenge, but you'll find that the 4:8 Principle is simple enough for even a child to learn. Even better news is that there is no need to be perfect. After all, perfection doesn't really exist apart from God. All you have to do is concentrate on progress. So as you read the upcoming pages, stop trying to be flawless, and instead, focus on daily improvement.

By deliberately working to improve your mental game, you will steadily upgrade every area of your life. Your family life will be more peaceful. You will hit your financial goals faster. With strong, toned mental muscles, you'll become more fit spiritually, emotionally, relationally, and physically. And along the way, you'll begin to enjoy life as it was meant to be—full of the joy that comes from trusting in God's promises.

What *Can* You Do?

When my son Ty was eight years old, he broke his right arm after his first football practice. He had been so excited after his first day of real contact that even before we got into the car to head home, he insisted on showing me, in slow motion, how he had learned to tackle. Unfortunately, he lost his balance and fell backward on his right arm, creating a buckle fracture just above his wrist. According to his doctor, Ty would have to be in a cast for at least six weeks to give the bone time to fully heal, and he would likely miss most of the games. This was not a good start to the fall.

> The mind is its own place and in itself can make a heaven of hell; a hell of heaven.
> — John Milton

After the initial disappointment, Ty seemed to be handling the setback fairly well. Then a couple of days later, while riding home from church, he went into a negative spiral, reciting everything he could not do with only one good arm. He was very thorough, even though his mother, Kristin, and I tried to interrupt him several times to break the self-defeating mental momentum.

When we arrived back at our house, I asked Ty to join me in my study for a few minutes. "Ty, don't you think there are lots of things you can still do, even with your broken right arm?" I asked.

"No, not the really good things," he replied skeptically.

"All right then," I said, "I'm going to give you a quick exercise, like I do in The 1% Club, that will show you how much you really can do."

Because he had no choice, Ty agreed to participate—unenthusiastically.

"Ty," I said, "write down twenty one things you can still do with just one arm, and we'll be done."

With a curious look, Ty responded, "Dad, I'm in a cast. I can't write."

"Oh, that's right," I said with a laugh, wishing we could start over. "Then you talk, Ty, and I'll write for you."

So Ty started talking, and I started writing. Slowly, with some prodding, the first few answers came. He could read books, ride his bike, watch TV, and play video games. Those things triggered even more ideas. Ty continued, "I could hike or run. I could play in my tree house. I could go to the movies, eat popcorn, and have M&M's. I could still do science experiments. I could do sit-ups, take a bath, and make my bed." As we approached the goal of twenty-one ideas, I was writing as fast as I could.

"Okay, that's twenty-one," I confirmed to Ty.

"Keep writing, Dad. I want to do some more," he said, no longer annoyed with the exercise.

Finally, with thirty-five answers, Ty was ready to stop. I handed him the list he had dictated and asked him to read it aloud. As he read, I could see the excitement growing. There really were a lot of things a kid could still do with a broken arm.

"Can I go show Mom my list?" Ty asked.

"Sure," I said, "but let me ask you one more question first. Ty, do you think we could have made just as long a list of the things you can't do with a broken arm?" I asked, hoping to create a coachable moment.

"Yes," he quickly answered, "but why in the world would we want to do that?"

"Good point," I said as I enjoyed his smile. "Go show Mom."

Over the next few days, I have to admit that Ty and I repeated an abbreviated version of that exercise several times whenever his attitude took a dive. Within a minute or two, though, Ty's mind-set quickly shifted back into positive gear. As the tension faded, you could see the joy return. Ty was learning how to win the battle of his mind and starting to understand the secret to a joy-filled life.

Your Thoughts Are Showing

Almost everything that happens to you, good or bad, originates with a single thought. Neuroscientists can now demonstrate that every thought sends electrical and chemical signals throughout your brain, ultimately affecting each cell in your body. Thoughts can influence your sleep, your digestion, your pulse, the chemical makeup of your blood, and all other bodily functions. **The secret conversations you hold in the privacy of your own mind are shaping your destiny, little by little.** With every thought that races through your mind, you are continually reinventing yourself and your future. Research indicates that the average person thinks approximately fifty thousand thoughts per day. This is either good or bad news because every thought moves you either toward your God-given potential or away from it. No thoughts are neutral.

> The outer world of circumstance shapes itself to the inner world of thought, and both pleasant and unpleasant external conditions are factors which make for the ultimate good of the individual. As the reaper of his own harvest, man learns both by suffering and bliss.
> – James Allen

11

Whatever you direct your mind to think about will ultimately be revealed for everyone to see. Remind yourself with a smile that *"my thoughts are showing."* See, you have two options: By your manner of thinking, you can draw out the best in yourself and others, or you can draw out the worst. **What you persistently think eventually but**

inevitably crystallizes into the words you speak and then the things you do.

Every thought you have shifts your life in a particular direction, sometimes in a minor way and sometimes in a major way. Every individual thought matters. Unfortunately, approximately 90 percent of the thoughts you have today are repeats from yesterday and the day before. This is the primary reason why effecting permanent, positive life improvement tends to be met with such stiff resistance in most people.

If your aim is to maximize your potential for joy, you must first discipline yourself mentally. This is your responsibility, something for which you must immediately take ownership. Do your part now so that God can honor your faith and empower you to live a life of excellence. Think the thoughts you would think if you trusted God's promises completely. Make the shift from random, reactive thinking to deliberate, purpose-driven thinking. You have authority over your thoughts, but God will not force you to exercise this aspect of your free will any more than he will compel you to exercise regularly, eat a healthy diet, read the Bible, or wear your seat belt. Right thinking is a choice you have to make for yourself the rest of your life. If you are committed, you can select your thoughts and thereby shape your life here on earth into something spectacular. The alternative is to give up this freedom and live a life of mediocrity dominated by uncertainty and suspense. This may sound harsh at first, but I know it is the truth—and I suspect you do as well.

In Romans 12:2, we are taught that transformation is the result of a renewed mind. The apostle Paul writes, "Do not conform any longer to the pattern of this world, but be transformed by the renewing of your mind. Then you will be able to test and approve what God's will is—his good, pleasing and perfect will" (NIV). The idea is that you have to retrain your thoughts and feelings if you want to experience God's ideal for your life and get the most out of every moment of every day. Unfortunately, most people struggle to change or renew their circumstances (lose weight, fix their marriage, make more money), when they should be asking God to help them renew their minds. When our minds are renewed, circumstances take care of themselves.

13

The happiness which brings enduring worth to life is not the superficial happiness that is dependent on circumstances. It is the happiness and contentment that fills the soul even in the midst of the most distressing circumstances and the most bitter environment. It is the kind of happiness that grins when things go wrong and smiles through the tears. The happiness for which our souls ache is one undisturbed by success or failure, one which will root deeply inside us and give inward relaxation, peace, and contentment, no matter what the surface problems may be. That kind of happiness stands in need of no outward stimulus.
– Billy Graham

The secret to living an exceptional life *tomorrow* is purely a matter of thinking strong, joyful thoughts *today*. It is the net result of programming your mind with the kind of high-quality ideas and boundless possibilities that will set you free and allow you to soar and thrive as God intends. I can't overemphasize the importance of developing mental discipline. The battle you wage against your human nature is an invisible one that will be won or lost in the mind. Minute by minute, hour by hour, in the hidden workshop of your mind, you are constructing thoughts of good or evil, depression or joy, success or failure. You are writing your own life story as a human being with each subtle and soundless thought you think.

The Gift of the Present

Did you know that you cannot be joy filled without thinking thoughts of joy? You cannot worry without thinking worrisome thoughts. You cannot be afraid without thinking thoughts of fear. Can you remember a time when you were thinking of hope and happiness but felt depressed at the same time? Can you imagine acting loving while thinking bitter thoughts of anger and resentment? While thinking, you have only the present moment. All you have is *now*. Think of it as the gift of the present! A blissful memory is experienced as present joy. A gloomy memory is experienced as present pain. As a result, **thinking, talking, and worrying about what you *don't* want can never bring you what you *do* want.**

The importance of right thinking is emphasized throughout the Old and New Testaments. In Proverbs, we are taught that "as [a person] thinks in his heart, so is he" (23:7, NKJV) and also that we must "keep [our] heart with all diligence, for out of it spring the issues of life" (4:23, NKJV). Protecting our minds from negative input will be the focus of part three.

In Job 3:25, we are warned that the things we intensely fear have a tendency to become reality. And Jesus repeatedly reminds us that what we receive will be the result of what we believe. He underscores this point in the Sermon on the Mount when he teaches that even to think lustful thoughts is a sin, yet if "your eye is good, your whole body is filled with light" (Matthew 6:22, NLT). In Matthew 15:18, we're taught that people are defiled or made unclean by what is in their hearts—in other words, by the way they think. Jesus knew well that persistent thoughts eventually lead to action. So did Paul, who encourages us to "take captive every thought to make it obedient to Christ" (2 Corinthians 10:5, NIV). Can you imagine a negative, cynical, self-defeating, or "woe is me" thought being obedient to Jesus Christ?

Finally, in the great simplicity of truth, James sums it up when he writes that one who doubts is "a double-minded man, unstable in all his ways" (James 1:8, NKJV). Being duplicitous or impure in your thinking is really the opposite of being mentally disciplined. It's like praying for sunshine and then grabbing your umbrella as you walk out the door. It is forgiving your spouse for a grievance and then repeatedly rehashing it in your mind. It is hoping for the best and secretly fearing the worst. It is the inability to direct your thoughts in a deliberate, preconceived direction. Though God's grace doesn't demand mental discipline, living a life of excellence must be preceded by it.

God designed your mind to be immensely powerful. This mental resource is one of the most wonderful blessings from our Creator. Even better, as part of your free will, he gave you command over your mind. This does not mean you *must* use this power, but it is available. This dominion over your thought life can be used to maximize your God-given potential, or it can be misused or even ignored. **The way you think can either multiply or shrink your gifts and talents.** How are you doing in this area? Up to this point in your life, have you been a faithful steward of your mental life?

The Bible clearly teaches that you will "reap what you sow." This is so simple that it is almost embarrassing to mention; however, it can be difficult to put into practice. We sow first, and then we reap. Nowhere is this more apparent than in our thinking. In Galatians 6:7 we are told, "Do not be deceived, God is not mocked; for whatever a man sows, that he will also reap" (NKJV). In 2 Corinthians 9:6, we are warned that if we sow sparingly, we will naturally also reap sparingly, but if we sow bountifully, we shall also reap bountifully. Our thoughts, like our actions, have consequences. **As relentlessly as you may try, you cannot think one thing and experience something else.** You cannot think critically about your spouse, even if you believe it is warranted, and reap true intimacy. You cannot think negatively and live positively any more than you can plant apple seeds and expect to harvest oranges. If you desire to live a joy-filled life—a life that fulfills God's purpose for you—you must keep your thoughts fixed on the things of God.

In chapter 2, you will learn how to create a fresh start and begin reaping the fruit of joyful thinking.

A Prayer for Joy

Lord,

Thank you for all the goodness in my life and the great plans you have for me, my family, and my future. I praise you for my healthy mind and the power you have instilled in my thoughts. Thanks especially for the freedom you have given me to select my thoughts and thereby influence my state of mind and my circumstances.

Help me to accept responsibility for my thinking. Lead me, moment by moment, to choose joyful thoughts that line up with the vision you have for my life. Protect me from searching for joy in all the wrong places, and inspire me to enjoy the gift of this present moment.

In Jesus' name,

Amen

This One Thing I Do . . .

Beginning today, I increase my *potential for joy* by identifying in writing one circumstance that I would like to improve and the change in thinking that must precede it.

CHAPTER 2

A NEW BEGINNING

Focusing on What Produces Joy

I believe the choice to be excellent begins with aligning your thoughts and words with the intention to require more from yourself.
– Oprah Winfrey

Even though we are free to choose what we think about, we often tell ourselves destructive things that limit—at least temporarily—the big things God wants to do through us. Pay attention to almost any conversation for about ten minutes and you will hear toxic self-talk, whining, commiserating, blaming, condemning, and justifying. You will hear people passionately arguing in favor of their most cherished limitations. Some insist that they are not being negative but realistic, giving an honest description of their lives. The rationalizations may be convincing, and most have become socially acceptable staples of speech, but when people violate Philippians 4:8, consequences, large or small, will always follow.

Where you have been, what you have done, and where you are now matters far less than where you are headed. If you persist in identifying with current or prior performance by constantly thinking and talking about it, then where you have been, where you are, and where you are going will all be one and the same. This holds true for your marriage, your business career, your golf game, and any other area of your life.

Paul's "To-Think" List

The basis for this book is the advice of the apostle Paul as recorded in Philippians 4:8, where he challenges us to seek out and dwell on the positives in our lives. When we look for places where God's character is revealed, we are reminded of his presence in our lives, and we are blessed.

Many people use "to-do" lists to clarify their priorities and guide them through the day. This is obviously a wise strategy, but even more important is a *"to-think" list.* In Philippians 4:8, Paul has essentially given us a *master* "to-think" list, illuminating the types of thoughts we should have if we want to produce positive results:

> Finally, brethren, whatsoever things are true, whatsoever things are honest, whatsoever things are just, whatsoever things are pure, whatsoever things are lovely, whatsoever things are of good report; if there be any virtue, and if there be any praise, think on these things. (Philippians 4:8, KJV)

In my workshops, for emphasis I display the last segment of Philippians 4:8 as rendered in the Amplified Bible:

> If there is any virtue and excellence, if there is anything worthy of praise, think on and weigh and take account of these things [fix your minds on them].

Consider this verse carefully for a moment. "Finally, brethren" is Bible talk for "In summary, folks" or "Let me break it down to the essence." The very fact that Paul is telling us what we should focus on reveals a critical point: We always have a choice. If we didn't, this verse would be unnecessary. If we were naturally positive all the time, Paul wouldn't emphasize this point so dramatically. If we could not control our negativity, this teaching would be unrealistic and beyond our capability.

Paul is reminding us that *we have a choice*. With God's help, we can control our thoughts. Further, his words teach us that the choice is between good and bad, between excellence and mediocrity. Life is never completely good or completely bad. **There will always be some junk, and there will always be some greatness.** Your marriage, your health, and your finances may be in outstanding condition, but you might be facing learning difficulties with one of your children. Maybe your kids are all thriving, but your marriage is in an exasperating rut. Or perhaps your family life is wonderful, but you're disappointed with your circle of friends, your weight, your faith, or the condition of your home. You will always have something to complain about, and you will always have some blessings to count.

Inevitably, life is filled with peaks and valleys. But even in the valleys, there will always be something working really well in your life; and even on the mountain peaks, everything will not be perfect. Life is always a mixture of good and bad.

Whether you choose to count your blessings or choose to complain, it's helpful to understand that *you have a choice*. This is true of life as a whole as well as in all the specific areas of life.

When you focus on the good, you not only notice more good but you actually *create* more good. Focusing on positive things causes you to search for more that's positive. As a result, you perceive and appreciate more good, which sets the stage for even more positive circumstances. Eventually, you will have more joy, more enthusiasm, and more gratitude. This outlook draws the best out of other people and situations, creating a *virtuous cycle* (rather than a vicious cycle) in which you continually find and multiply what you're looking for.

In Philippians 4:8, we learn that

- There will always be some junk (something worth complaining about).
- There will always be some good stuff (something to be grateful for).
- We can exercise our free will (choosing either positive or negative).

When you focus on the negative, what happens? Review (but don't dwell on) the following list of self-defeating thoughts:

Forty Junk-Producing Thoughts

1. I'm *never* going to be that happy again.
2. That's just the way it is.
3. This probably won't work.
4. If I had money, I'd just worry about losing it.

5. I don't have what it takes.

6. That *always* happens.

7. The honeymoon is officially over.

8. I hate myself.

9. He doesn't love me anymore.

10. I am not worthy.

11. I'm just not creative.

12. I could *never* do that.

13. My back is *always* going out.

14. I have to accept my limitations.

15. I can *never* say that right.

16. That makes me sick.

17. I'm *never* going to remember his name.

18. I don't need this.

19. I can't.

20. That's typical for me.

21. If such and such happens, I'm going to be *sooo* mad.

22. It's *never* going to work out.

23. I knew my marriage wasn't going to work out.

24. We can't agree on anything.

25. It isn't my fault.

26. I used to have so much energy.

27. That's just my luck.

28. That's just who I am.

29. We're just growing apart.

30. I *always* seem to dip into my savings.

31. It's *never* going to be like it used to be.

32. I'm not attractive to him anymore.

33. That's out of my price range. I'll never be able to afford it.

34. She doesn't understand me.
35. I'm living proof of Murphy's Law.
36. I'll just have to put up with this.
37. *Nothing* good ever happens to me.
38. Everything I eat goes straight to my waist.
39. *Nobody* wants to pay me what I'm worth.
40. It's hopeless.

Have you ever said these statements to yourself or heard somebody else say them? Maybe not the exact words, but something close—perhaps even more egregious than those I just listed. When you think careless thoughts, you can count on missing many of the blessings that God has in store for you.

Fortunately, you are not limited to thinking in only one way. You can choose from an infinite number of potential thoughts. Because your thinking is not fixed, it can constantly be improved when you make the commitment to do so. Remember, **each moment is a new beginning.** Your future is not defined by your past. Your thoughts can change, and consequently, your future life can become totally different. Negative thinking corrupts your brain and triggers harmful mental states such as anxiety, moodiness, depression, and irritability. Unless you train your mind constructively, your thinking becomes automatic, impulsive, and often erroneous. Your thoughts often misrepresent reality by *bending, distorting, deleting, exaggerating,* or otherwise *manipulating* the truth. We will explore these concepts in depth in chapter 6.

In fact, most negative thinking is simply a bundle of lies that cannot be substantiated and certainly could not make it through a vigorous cross-examination. When you think a limiting thought without challenging it, your mind buys into it. To counteract this, remind yourself that negative thoughts do not come from God. God is positive to everything but sin. If a thought brings about worry, fear, or fatigue, it is not from God. After all, the Bible tells us, "God has not given us a spirit of fear, but of power and of love and of a sound mind" (2 Timothy 1:7, NKJV). If a thought leads you to feel like a victim instead of a victor, it is not from God. Paul also tells us, "Thanks be to God! He gives us the victory through our Lord Jesus Christ" (1 Corinthians 15:57, NIV). Though we are engineered for success, it is very easy to inadvertently program ourselves for mediocrity if we neglect to think positive, goal-directed thoughts. Productive thinking and destructive thinking are both merely habits.

Compare the list of joy-producing thoughts below with the previous list of self-defeating thoughts. Life is too short to be negative! As long as you have a choice, why not exercise your free will and choose the higher thoughts? Review these and see if you agree with me.

Forty Joy-Producing Thoughts

1. I expect the best, and it shows!
2. I trust God; my faith is strong.
3. I am responsible.
4. I take deliberate action to reach my goals.
5. I now accept the best that life has to offer.
6. I am a new creature through Christ!
7. My metabolism works effectively.

8. I stay lean even as I age.
9. I believe in the most perfect outcome of every challenge in my life.
10. I'll figure out how to earn it.
11. I am healthy and strong.
12. I have boundless energy!
13. I surround myself with winners.
14. I experience abundance now and forever.
15. God has great plans for me!
16. I am grateful for my unshakable faith.
17. Everything I need, I already have.
18. My brain works perfectly.
19. With God, my future keeps getting better.
20. My memory is crisp and vivid.
21. I change what I need to change.
22. I let go and let God.
23. I'm making progress.
24. I control my thoughts.
25. I am transformed by the renewing of my mind.
26. I pray for others.
27. With Christ, I am unstoppable.
28. I can improve this situation.
29. I ask, and I receive.
30. I learn Scripture easily.
31. I am supercharged with joy.
32. I am ready for a breakthrough.
33. Day by day my marriage is growing stronger.
34. I act consistently with my faith.
35. I am bold.
36. I am lovable.

37. I think about what is good, just, and gracious.
38. I am learning a lot through this experience.
39. My lifestyle supports unshakable faith.
40. I surrender myself and my future to God, and I trust him.

Do you want a future that is better than your present? No matter how blessed you feel at the moment, I still trust you answered an enthusiastic *yes!* I believe God has awesome plans for you. I may not know you personally yet, but I believe God wants to do exciting things through all of his children, and that includes you.

If you're with me so far, let me coach you for a moment. Dig a little deeper, using these follow-up questions:

- Would you like to grow in your faith?
- Would you like to overcome a particular heartache?
- Would you like to break out of a tiresome rut?
- Do you want to get closer to your spouse?
- Would you like to develop a Christlike character?
- Would you like to have even greater influence in the lives of your children?
- Do you aspire to higher levels of physical energy and vitality?
- Would you like to be more emotionally resilient?
- Would you like to be in a stronger position financially?
- Would you like to overcome a specific self-defeating habit?
- Would you like to make a bigger difference in your business or in your community?
- Would you like to be joy filled?

I imagine you answered yes to most of the preceding questions. We all want to experience a fuller, deeper, more meaningful life. But how do we actually reach that goal? And what does our thinking have to do with it?

The 4:8 Principle

If you want your future to be different from the present, then *The 4:8 Principle* was written with you in mind. If you want your future to be just a little better than your life now, you will need to change your thinking just a little. **If you desire a future that is a lot better than your present, you will need to change a lot about the way you think.** Maybe you want a little change in your finances and a big change in your marriage. Maybe you want to get into a little better shape physically, but you want to grow a lot closer to God. Whatever improvement you are looking for must start with your thoughts.

You'd never invite a thief into your house. So why would you allow thoughts that steal your joy to make themselves at home in your mind?

Based on Philippians 4:8, the 4:8 Principle states that **whatever you give your attention to expands in your experience.**

Consider what happens in a theater or stadium when a spotlight is turned on. Your awareness shifts to the object underneath the light. As you give attention to the highlighted performance, you cease paying attention to what is left in the dark. The last time we took our kids to the circus, I wit-

28

nessed this scenario firsthand. As the spotlight was aimed at one or two of the three rings, the "unused ring" was left in complete darkness. I had to strain a bit, but as I looked closely at the unlit ring, I could see the stage crew, dressed in black, making preparation for the next stunt. Like the circus production, you will always have some degree of darkness in your life, but you can choose where you focus your spotlight. Remember, whatever is not under the light has far less significance.

Dwelling on something means
- Thinking deeply
- Reviewing
- Replaying
- Meditating
- Mulling it over
- Talking about it

This is the essence of the 4:8 Principle: **If you dwell on your strengths, your blessings, your goals, and all the people who love you, then you will attract even more blessings, even more love, and even more accomplishments.** Everything you need to be joy-filled, you already have!

Reflexively, you will tend to dwell on either what you fear or what most excites you. In the absence of a clear, compelling vision, you and I are more likely to descend into fear thinking and away from 4:8 Thinking. You can build any virtue into your mentality by dwelling on that virtue every single day. For example, if you need to develop patience, meditate on patience each day and visualize your patient responses to the upcoming situations you will encounter. Whatever you give your attention to will be elevated in your consciousness.

The more frequently you think about something, the tighter the grip it exerts on you, the decisions you make, and the actions you take.

Because no one else can think for you, this is your responsibility. The 4:8 Principle is about optimizing what is within your control. Until you can proactively determine what you are going to think about, you will never quite grasp the fullness of joy that God intends for you.

Can you imagine Paul's advice in reverse? It might go something like this:

> Finally, folks, whatever is untrue, dishonest, unjust, impure, ugly, negative, vicious, or worthy of criticism, think about these things.

Not exactly the type of advice you would like to pass on to your children, is it? You might laugh when you read it, but there are quite a few people who seem to be following the spoof more than the real advice. Remember that dwelling on your problems doesn't fix them; it just makes you an expert on them. Due to our human nature, **we live in a society bent on highlighting what is wrong with just about everything.** This is so common that most people hardly notice it anymore. Good news does not make the front page. A 70 percent chance of sunshine is expressed as a 30 percent chance of rain. A dictatorship can be defeated, yet a lack of perfect peace is likely to be the big story. An unprecedented election occurs in Afghanistan, and newspapers around the world make "Possible Voter Fraud" the headline.

Churchgoers walk out of Sunday morning services like Broadway critics, discussing what they did and did not like about the sermon rather than considering what God was trying to say to them through that message. Kids bring home report cards with some A's, some B's, and a C, and parents blabber about the C as if the better grades didn't exist. It is possible, if you focus on it, to find fault with just about anything or anyone.

Aiming Your Spotlight

The vast majority of people want a better life in one way or another, yet they struggle with how to get from where they are now to where they would like to be. Let me give you a few examples: Jim wants to earn more money to provide for his family better, but he continues to think about his business as a burden. Instead of practicing 4:8 Think-

> Let your light so shine before men, that they may see your good works and glorify your Father in heaven.
> — Matthew 5:16, NKJV

ing by using his discretionary time to become more valuable in the marketplace, he squanders it complaining about his inadequate compensation. He secretly thinks, *When they start paying me more, I'll start being more valuable.* Jim is turning the spotlight on the wrong thing.

Susan wants a closer relationship with her husband,

Chris, but she constantly reminds herself of the reasons why that will likely never happen. Rather than expecting and then planning for the best in her marriage, she is mentally retreating and resigning herself to a future of disappointment. Susan is also aiming the spotlight on the wrong target.

What about you? Is there an area of your life where you are pointing the spotlight in the wrong direction?

When you activate the 4:8 Principle in your own life, you begin to see opportunities where there were previously only obstacles. It's not that the difficulties disappeared; your focus has simply shifted to the resolution. The 4:8 Principle challenges you to approach the inevitable setbacks and sorrows of life with a positive and forward-looking perspective that allows you to deal with them effectively. Instead of exhaustively redescribing your problems, the 4:8 Principle counsels you to marinate in the *solutions* to your problems.

In your own personal growth, your thinking guides you down a path of either comfort or character. In your marriage, your thinking determines whether you bring out the best or the worst in your spouse. As a parent, your thinking about your children and their future amplifies their potential or smothers it. In your spiritual walk, you will have either a shallow or a deep experience of God, depending on your thinking. In your business, you prosper only to the ceiling that your thoughts permit. Assuredly, your only limitations are the ones you think you have.

As you incorporate the 4:8 Principle into your day-to-day life, you will become more attuned to your thinking and will realize how much productive energy is squandered through unconsciously scattered thought patterns. You will notice how well-established, sloppy mental habits tend to shift you from forward into reverse throughout the day, resulting in little net progress.

When you bring your thinking into the domain of your conscious, creative control, you will rapidly discover what an enormous advantage you have in sculpting the conditions of your life. In the upcoming chapters, I will show you exactly how to release the power of the 4:8 Principle on a daily basis. For now, though, I want to share with you the simplest method for redirecting your thoughts onto what is worthwhile, constructive, and joy producing.

Ask 4:8 Questions

The most effective technique for instilling the habit of 4:8 Thinking is developing the habit of asking, re-asking, and then answering 4:8 Questions. **A 4:8 Question is a question about your life that extracts a positive response.** I'll share additional 4:8 Questions with you throughout the upcoming chapters and in the Afterword, but here are five examples to help you get the idea:

- What are five things I am thankful for right now?
- What are five of my strengths or positive traits?
- What are five of my best achievements so far?
- Who are the five people who love me the most?
- What five things am I looking forward to in the next seven days?

Each of the questions above demands a positive answer, and by asking for five answers to each, I am compelling you to *dwell* on the positive. It is important to note that damage isn't caused by the fleeting negative thought but rather by the negative thought that sets up shop in your mind. After all, you cannot completely control the thoughts that are triggered from your surroundings, but **you can unquestionably control what you choose to dwell on.**

Imagine a spark from a campfire flying onto your sweater. As long as you quickly brush it away, it will do no harm. It is the same way with negative thoughts. Train yourself to become aware of them, and then sweep them away without much fanfare.

The 4:8 Questions are a simple tool to displace negativity in the short term and help you take conscious control of your repeated thoughts.[1] These questions then divert your attention to the best things in your life.

4:8 Questions = 4:8 Thinking = Joy-Filled Living

You'll find that 4:8 Questions immediately change what you're focusing on. Consequently, they affect how you feel, as well as your level of creativity, excitement, and joy at any given moment.

To get these questions working for you, put a copy where you can see them often, such as on a bathroom mirror, a night table, your computer screen, the refrigerator, or the steering wheel of your car. You could make a screen saver containing your 4:8 Questions or tape them to your

---

[1] To request a free set of four bookmarks with 4:8 Questions listed on them, please visit www.tommynewberry.com, and we will send them for you to use and share with friends. A special version just for kids is also included.

treadmill or exercise bike. The point here is to keep them "top of mind" as much as possible throughout the day. I open most of my workshops using 4:8 Questions similar to those on page 33. I recommend that you start your day with these questions as well. I answer these questions in the shower each morning; that way, they don't take any extra time. One of my clients practices answering these questions at dinnertime before grace. Other members of The 1% Club cover these 4:8 Questions as they drift to sleep.

Anti-4:8 Questions

Alternatively, you are free to ask questions such as the ones below. But as my son put it, "why in the world would you want to do that?"

- What are five things that make my life really stink right now?
- What are five of my most damaging weaknesses?
- What are my top five recent mistakes or blunders?
- Who are five people who would really like to see me fail or suffer?
- What are five inevitable things that I am absolutely dreading in the next seven days?

It is so common to minimize what is working well and exaggerate what is not working. The downside of human nature quietly nudges us to accentuate what is missing and downplay what is available. It is easy to get consumed with the obstacles and forget about the goals. It is so easy to entertain hostile, turbulent thoughts about the future and miss the gift of the present. But when you actively practice the 4:8

Principle, you will spotlight the positive aspects of your past, present, and future. The cumulative effect of this new mind-set will excite you as well as those around you.

You may be wondering if there is a time to be negative. The answer is a definite yes. And that time is before you read this book! With *The 4:8 Principle* as your guide, you are ready to slam the door on negativity and say good-bye to idle, limiting thoughts once and for all.

A Prayer for a Fresh Start

Dear heavenly Father,

Thank you for new beginnings! Infuse me today with a fresh dose of your Holy Spirit, and fill me with thoughts that strengthen my character and cause me to grow fully into the image you intended for me when you brought me into this world. Help me preoccupy my mind with thoughts of you, with thoughts that are pure, true, lovely, and worthy of praise. Heighten my awareness so that my thinking doesn't unconsciously drift into the negative, limiting, and counterproductive patterns that ensnare so many.

Protect me from the temptation to complain, condemn, or focus on what's wrong with things. Instead, elevate my thinking and open my eyes so that I see your presence in all situations. I want to appreciate the abundance that surrounds me and activate the joy that is hidden within me.

In Jesus' name,

Amen

This One Thing I Do . . .

Beginning today, I increase my potential for joy by asking and answering the 4:8 Questions (listed on page 33) when I wake up in the morning and before I fall asleep at night.

THE CIRCUS ELEPHANTS

When I was a kid, one of my coaches told me a story about circus elephants. When these elephants are still little and weak, they are chained to iron stakes in the ground, which prevent them from breaking free and running away. This allows the circus trainers to keep them close, work with them, and prepare them for their routines. What's strange is that even after the little elephants grow into huge, powerful animals capable of lifting a ton or more with their trunks, they remain restricted by those same miniature stakes in the ground. Even when they are more than strong enough to yank the stake out of the ground and roam free, they don't do it. They don't even try. They remain limited by the old boundaries. Sometimes we demonstrate this type of helplessness as well. We focus on that little stake (or *mistake*) from our past and forget that, with God's help, we have the power to release whatever has been holding us back.

CHAPTER 3

WOW, THAT'S ME!

Embracing Your God-Given Identity

I shut my eyes in order to see.
– Paul Gauguin

Every night as I tuck my older boys into bed, I remind each one that he is a beautiful, wonderful child of God. I've done this since I was still rocking them to sleep in their nursery. It didn't take long before they completed these very significant words for me. I would say, "You are a beautiful—" and they would proudly cut me off and add, "wonderful child of God." Even when I traveled, I would call at bedtime whenever I could and repeat this ritual with them. Before long, we added to the list of positive nighttime declarations:

- Mom and Dad love you forever, always, no matter what.
- You love God more than anything else in the whole world.
- You respect and obey your mother and father.
- You think for yourself.

- You make wise choices.
- Actions have consequences.
- You have courage.

My first words to my newest and youngest son, Brooks, were, "You're a beautiful, wonderful child of God! Welcome to the world!"

My boys have been told "You are a beautiful, wonderful child of God" so many times that they often repeat it in their sleep. Hard to believe? Don't feel bad—my wife didn't believe me, either, when I first told her. One evening when I was running late, I found that my oldest son, who was four at the time, was already asleep. Always curious about the subconscious, I had to try an experiment. I leaned over, right above Ty's ear, and whispered, "You are a beautiful, wonderful—" Without opening his eyes or acknowledging my presence, he continued "—child of God." I almost fell over, but I could not resist trying it again. This time I stopped after saying, "You are a—" and he instantly whispered back to me "—beautiful, wonderful child of God."

That was not enough for me. Now I needed a witness! I rushed into our bedroom and asked Kristin to come see for herself. Despite being a bit skeptical, she hurried back into Ty's room with me. With Kristin watching closely, I started with, "You are a beautiful—" I paused and waited for him to finish, but nothing happened. Not even a sound. I tried it again, but still he made no response. I was starting to fear it was going to be like the "repair-guy syndrome"—the technician shows up to fix an appliance and then it starts working (until he leaves). Fortunately, on my third try, Ty came through for me just as he had done before. To his mother's amazement, he again affirmed in his sleep that he was indeed a beautiful, wonderful child of God.

The apostle John confirms this truth when he writes, "How great is the love the Father has lavished on us, that we should be called children of God!" (1 John 3:1, NIV). We are children of God—but we don't always view ourselves that way. Your self-concept refers to the way you customarily think about yourself, and it either expands or restricts your potential for joy.

As I emphasized in chapter 1, when you change your focus, your circumstances change soon thereafter—presuming, of course, that you retain your new way of thinking. (Expecting circumstances to improve as the result of only a temporary elevation in thinking would be like a farmer expecting to harvest a crop he planted only last week.) This doesn't happen overnight, as a rule, but nonetheless, it happens much sooner than you might expect.

With each seed of thought, your self-concept shifts toward your highest potential or away from it. When you fine-tune your thinking to conform to Philippians 4:8, you naturally begin to view yourself and others with much greater respect. Why? Because you're focusing on people's positive traits rather than judging them or concentrating on their negatives.

Too many people resign themselves to lives far below what God intended. They don't see themselves as worthy. For some, this insecurity may manifest itself in their marriage; for others, it's in their finances; and for others, it's in their life as a whole. As a result, instead of working to grow and advance, they cope with a "barely-get-by, grin-and-bear-it" approach to life. I don't want that for you! In this chapter, you will learn the power of your self-concept in helping you live a joy-filled life.

You Are His Masterpiece!

Do you see yourself as a child of almighty God? **Remember *whose* you really are.** You are an original masterpiece. In fact, the Bible uses these exact words to describe us! "We are God's masterpiece. He has created us anew in Christ Jesus, so we can do the good things he planned for us long ago" (Ephesians 2:10, NLT). There has never been and never will be anyone just like you, and God has not made anyone else in the world out of better clay than he used to make you. Your life here on earth is your special, unrepeatable opportunity to fulfill God's vision for your life and to magnify the joy he has placed within you. Recognize that the true you is not your flesh and bones. You are a spiritual being living a temporary human experience—a dress rehearsal for eternity. Why not see yourself as joy filled as God created you to be? Remember that joy is an outward sign of inward faith in God's promises. So, by magnifying the joy God has given you, you also exhibit your faith to others and encourage them.

Any permanent progress in life starts on the inside and spreads to the outside. Attempted improvement that begins externally is doomed for failure in the long run. Why? All lasting growth begins with changes to the mental images you hold inside your head. They ultimately spread to the outside and create permanent changes in your circumstances. This is part of God's perfect design.

Much discouragement and underachievement result from dwelling on the failings of our human nature. A mediocre *self-concept* does not come from God but from the stains of the world. It comes from seeing ourselves different from how God sees us. It results from continuing to identify with and claim the things that haven't worked. It comes from continuing to think about ourselves as unworthy, as if we've forgotten about the blood of Jesus Christ that cleanses and purifies us. *This certainly violates the 4:8 Principle.*

43

When you remind yourself of your true identity, you will find it much easier to live according to Philippians 4:8 and filter out the junk that steals your joy. Likewise, when you practice the 4:8 Principle, it is far easier to accept yourself as a kid of the King. When you see yourself as a child of God, you do not accept artificial restrictions on the quantity of joy or the level of impact you can have in this world. That's critical because how you perceive yourself sets the ceiling for what God can do with you. When you see yourself as down and defeated, that is what you will surely be. This woeful approach does you no good personally and only serves to minimize your contribution in the world. However, **if you choose to see yourself as more than a conqueror through Christ (see Romans 8:37), you will certainly ascend to that level.**

Deciding the value you will place on yourself is another key choice you have to make. Many people allow this decision to be made for them by their dominant exposures—books, media, and other people, for example—which we will discuss in chapters 7 and 8. When you consider the stakes, that approach is quite a gamble. Why not agree with your Creator, and see yourself through his eyes?

You can never outgrow your self-concept; you can only replace it. When you do, your potential for joy will be unlimited, and your life will never again be the same!

Understand Your "Joy Software"

In many ways, your brain works like a computer. When you receive positive or negative input about yourself, you store it in your subconscious mind and later express those messages in your feelings and behaviors. The way you perceive and organize those inputs exerts a strong influence on how you interact with others. Unless you are taught how to reject the negative messages, you will tend to accept them as the truth. As I mentioned earlier, most people never challenge their own thinking. Instead, they respond to negative thoughts as if they came from God, when in reality they might be erroneous, irrational, or warped. Accepting these thoughts at face value leads to behavior that is rooted in error. Because we're typically not taught to question the validity of our self-concept, we simply behave as if it were true.

Because of the obvious correlations between the brain and a computer, I've found it helpful with my clients to discuss *self-concept* in familiar computer terms. So, for example, if your brain is the hardware, it follows that your mind (or your thought patterns) would be the software. If you can understand your thought patterns, you can also learn how to upgrade them so they will be more and more effective. I am going to give you both the understanding and the tools to upgrade your mental software to the next release and beyond, allowing you to experience more joy and positively affect more people.

Your self-concept is quite simply your impression of yourself as a human being. Though it is chiefly an unconscious mental construct, its influence on who you become over the course of your life is very real. Your self-concept is your distinctive combination of convictions, assumptions, life experiences, memories, feelings, and dreams for the future that are all bundled together to fashion the image that you hold of yourself. If you become consciously aware of your self-concept, you can refine it to your advantage and tap into more of your potential. If, like most people, you're not aware of it, it is likely to work to your disadvantage and diminish your capacity for growth, contribution, and joy.

The power of the self-concept is found in two passages from Scripture. One is in Proverbs 27:19, where Solomon advises, "As water reflects a face, so a man's heart reflects the man" (NIV). The second is found in Matthew 7:20, where Jesus says, "Just as you can identify a tree by its fruit, so you can identify people by their actions" (NLT). These verses clearly show that what you observe in your own life is merely a reflection of what is going on in your mental software. What we do externally reflects what we are really like and what we are thinking internally.

The greatest news that I can give you about your self-concept is that you were not born with it. You have acquired it as you progressed through life—and that means you can

45

change it if you want to and if you learn how. As your coach, I can't make you want to improve it, but I can show you how.

Picture inside a Picture

Do you have a PiP function on your television? That's the picture-in-picture feature that allows you to watch two programs at once. I suppose this is for people who can't be satisfied with just one program at a time. The function creates a small picture in the upper right-hand corner of your screen, allowing you to watch a program on another channel while you are watching the primary game or program on the main screen. Initially, this special feature was promoted to football fans who wanted to keep track of a second game. Now, in our digital age, it serves all sorts of "critical" TV needs.

Get this TV image in your mind. Your self-concept has a lot of similarities with this PiP function. It consists of three elements, all of which operate behind the scenes at the unconscious level. The first is your *self-ideal,* or *future picture,* which is the perfect vision you hold of yourself and what you hope to achieve at some distant point in your lifetime. The next is your *self-image,* or *current picture,* which is how you see yourself today. Finally, there is your *self-worth,* which is the private reputation you hold of yourself. Your future picture is like that game you're watching up in the corner of the screen—the picture within the picture. You pay very little attention to it. Your current picture is the game that is going on right now, the program taking up most of the screen. This holds most of your interest. Your self-worth

46

predetermines what channels or programs you give yourself permission to watch.

As long as the current game is interesting, you will keep watching it. If the game in the upper right-hand corner is no better or even less exciting than the game you are currently watching, you'll watch the current game indefinitely. That annoying little picture box will never be expanded. But if the game in the corner starts to get really compelling, you will click on the remote to make that picture take up the whole screen.

A fundamental reason why so many people are living far beneath their potential for joy is that there is little difference between the two "games" on the screen of their self-concept. There's no substantive difference between their current self image and the vision they have for their future. This shouldn't be the case! As God's child, the future he has planned for you is a definite *wow!* "'For I know the plans I have for you,' declares the LORD, 'plans to prosper you and not to harm you, plans to give you hope and a future'" (Jeremiah 29:11, NIV).

> Your self-concept has three aspects:
>
> 1. Self-ideal
> 2. Self-image
> 3. Self-worth

Your future picture is exciting; you can count on it. But you've got to do your part. You have a responsibility to ask for the vision. Then you must polish that vision into something so irresistible that you are impatiently searching for the remote to press that little button and fill up the full screen with the "other game." If you have no clear vision, your potential for joy can rapidly disintegrate.

Your future picture is your best-case scenario. It is the future you, upgraded and better than ever. When this future vision is divinely inspired, it will pull you over, around, or through any wall of comfort or fear that may be temporarily blocking your way.

48

Let's look at the three distinct components of your self-concept in a little more detail.

Your Self-Ideal

Again, the first element of your self-concept is called your *self-ideal*, which is the future picture you have of yourself. It is your best-case scenario of the person that you can become. It is not necessarily accurate; rather, it reflects what you *believe* is ultimately possible for you to become and do. It is what you now consider to be your best future. Your self-ideal is what your life would look like if everything were perfect for you. It is a composite of all your goals, dreams, aspirations, and role models combined into a singular vision that is best thought of as your future picture.

Though everyone has a self-ideal, only a few are consciously aware of it. The self-ideal provides feedback for you as you trek through life. **Like a personal GPS device, your self-ideal prompts you unconsciously to "turn here, turn there" as you navigate your way to your future destination.** Because your self-ideal unites your past experiences with your hopes for the future, it can serve to restrict you. Like the circus elephants, you may be chained to an outdated self-ideal that should have expired years ago.

Most people have not consciously created their self-ideal, and therefore, it has developed haphazardly. If it lacks intentionality, it will be vague and unclear. And if it's unclear, your brain won't work to make it happen. Up to this point in your life, has your self-ideal been developed by design or by default?

The self-ideal is an intangible concept. It's a mental construct. One of the best ways to make the self-ideal both more concrete and more positive is to develop a detailed personal mission statement. This is a conscious, written articulation of your full potential *as God sees it*. With a mission statement, you take this intangible construct of the self-ideal and turn it into something concrete. Your mission statement, along with your lifetime goals, becomes a physical tool you can use to fine-tune the image that you have of yourself in the future.[2]

Like your self-concept as a whole, you were not born with a self-ideal—which means you can transform it. Starting this conversion will be the focus of chapter 4.

Your Self-Image

Formed primarily from your environmental influences, which we'll cover in the last section of this book, your current self-image is the subconscious mechanism responsible for guiding your behavior. From the PiP example on pages 46–47, it is the game that's going on *now*, based primarily on

[2] I strongly encourage you to develop a personal mission statement, which is an excellent tool in many ways. For an effective, step-by-step approach, see my book *Success Is Not an Accident*.

your interactions with others. It develops from what you say to yourself and what others—particularly your parents and spouse—say to you. You have an overall self-image, but you also have subsidiary self-images that influence your marriage, your parenting, your fitness, your faith.

Our self-image is critical because **we almost always act consistently with the internal image we have of ourselves.** In fact, you cannot expect to behave different from your self-image programming any more than you could expect to put chocolate cake batter in the oven and an hour later take out an apple pie. You get out only what you put in. You can override it, but it takes a conscious, deliberate effort to do so.

Your mental image of yourself acts like a performance thermostat, regulating your behavior just as a thermostat controls room temperature. It sets the upper and lower limits on the quality of your performance within each area of your life as well as your life as a whole. You can walk over to the wall and change the thermostat anytime you want—if you are willing to do it. If you do not change your performance thermostat, you are very likely to keep repeating what you have always done. In the next chapter, you will learn eight steps that will change your "thermostat."

Your self-image feeds you repetitive rationalizations that keep you entrenched in your current circumstances. You will hear things such as these:

- Just start the diet (or workout) tomorrow.
- She should apologize to you first.
- You can catch up next week.

- Better to play it safe.
- What cannot be cured must be endured.
- One more time won't hurt anything.
- You're an imposter.

Because your self-image is wired to your short-term emotional appetite, you will hardly ever *feel* like acting in a manner *inconsistent* with this self-image set point. However, there is a solution: **You can override past negative programming by deliberately choosing new behaviors that line up with your God-given potential, whether or not you feel like it.**

Your self-image, or inner mirror, determines how you use your time, talents, knowledge, skills, and experiences. Did you catch that last sentence? I think it explains one of the great mysteries of life. Why do many gifted and often well-educated individuals fail to live up to their potential? In many more cases than we might like to acknowledge, it is because they see themselves as losers instead of winners. We all know lots of folks who have great talent but do little with it. On the other hand, we know plenty of people who have few advantages but who make the most of them.

Wow, That's Me!

Think of a recent peak moment, a time when everything went as well as or better than you had hoped and you felt at your best. Maybe it was a certain evening with your spouse when you really connected and felt closer than ever before. Perhaps it was last weekend on the tennis court or golf course when you were playing your "A" game. Maybe it was a super-successful day in the office when you delivered your best presentation or earned your largest check.

From time to time, we all have these success experiences. How we process them is a valuable indicator of our self-image. If the peak moment exceeded our expectations, we will often discount the experience and assign it to good luck, fortunate timing, or "the Imposter."

You know the Imposter! He is the imaginary individual who, if you let him, hogs the credit for your best moments. Of course, it's just another mental trick performed by a negative self-image, which results in blocking your growth. The Imposter is an inner voice that tries to persuade you that, despite the evidence to the contrary, you are "playing over your head." You don't really have the skills to handle the situation you're in; if you accomplish something good, it is due to luck. **The truth is that these peak moments, when you appear to be playing over your head, are actually glimpses of your full potential.** Why not turn things upside down and consider that the deep connection with your spouse, that day of excellence on the golf course, that big check are all a direct result of *who you really are*? **What if we attributed not our best moments but our worst moments to the Imposter?**

Unfortunately, we tend to *distance* ourselves from our best moments, explaining them away as "exceptions to the rule," with the rule being our current picture of ourselves.

> What you see is what you get.

On the other hand, if we have a rough day on the golf course, a bad day in the office, or a turbulent evening with our spouse, we tend to *overidentify* with that experience and think, *This must be the true me.*

The mental difference between a weekend warrior and a world-class athlete illustrates this dynamic clearly. The weekend warrior, or amateur athlete, goes out on the golf course, shoots his lowest score ever, and then dissolves that breakthrough with comments like these:

- "Wow, I must be lucky today."
- "I guess it will catch up with me next time."
- "I wish I could play like this every time."

Weekend warriors tend to distance themselves from their best performance and the positive change that could take place. World-class athletes, on the other hand, have a bad day on the course and instantly shrug it off, attributing it to the Imposter. They detach themselves from an unacceptable performance with comments like these:

- "I know the real me, and that wasn't it."
- "Wow, that is so unlike me."
- "I'll be playing my 'A' game tomorrow."

The next time you goof something up in your life—you have a frustrating day or an awful minute—just tell yourself that it must be the Imposter. Then remind yourself of your true potential. Remind yourself of what is lovely, true, gracious, and worthy of praise . . . about you.

To experience joy to the fullest, you need to think like a world-class athlete and overidentify with your best self, with those times when you feel unstoppable. The next time you sense your marriage is on a roll, reinforce it privately with *This is just a glimpse of how good it could be all the time.* **The next time you have a breakthrough, remind yourself, *Wow, that's me!***

Your Self-Worth

We've already looked at the future picture *(self-ideal)* and the current picture *(self-image)*. I call the third component of your self-concept your *self-worth*. In the earlier television example, I said your self-worth determines what programs you give yourself permission to watch in the first place. This is just another way of saying that in this world, you will receive only what you are willing to let in. If you feel insecure and think of yourself as inadequate and undeserving, then those very thoughts will get in the way of your full potential. Your self-worth demonstrates how spiritually fit and ready to do God's work you really are. It also reveals how receptive you are to God's blessings and favor. **Self-worth is authentic self-esteem rooted in your uniqueness as a child of God.** You recognize that you are a special, unrepeatable miracle, "fearfully and wonderfully made" (Psalm 139:14, NIV). You accept that God has great plans for your life. You trust God's Word more than the words of others to appraise your value as a person. "What is man that you are mindful of him, the son of man that you care for him? You made him a little lower than the heavenly beings and crowned him with glory and honor" (Psalm 8:4-5, NIV).

Self-worth is not based on achievements but on the significance you place on your life outside of your performance—on your identity as one created and loved by God. Oddly enough, when you see yourself as worthwhile and valuable outside of any accomplishments, you are better positioned to excel.

Typically, the strongest self-worth develops in childhood with kids who perceive unconditional love from their parents. This unconditional love imitates God's love and grace and is expressed to kids most straightforwardly through concepts like the following:

55

- **Absolute truth** instead of *relative truth*
  Emphasize the Word of God.
  Unambiguously communicate right and wrong.
  De-emphasize political correctness.
- **Positive affirmation** instead of *destructive criticism*
  "You have what it takes!"
  "Mom and Dad are very proud of you!"
  "No matter what you do, we still love you."
- **Wise limits** instead of *trendy boundaries*
  This is allowable; this is not.
  Character building matters most.
  Inspect what you expect. Accountability is critical.

Children who grow up with absolute truth, positive affirmation, and wise limits tend to become authentic adults who are comfortable in their own skin. There's also a bonus here: Kids with high self-worth are likely to be high performers. In fact, nothing will improve your child's performance like an injection of self-worth. Without the stress of posing and pretending, they have more fuel and focus for achieving the goals they find most worthwhile.

The same is true for you. The most well-adjusted, mature individuals have a high sense of self-worth, which means they say yes only to things they feel terrific about. They do what they love for a living. They have fun at it. And they succeed more often than not because they are so relaxed and comfortable with themselves. They don't need to prove anything.

Most parents love their children unconditionally. What matters, though, is whether or not the child *perceives* this. If a child senses that she will have to earn her parents' love through good grades, recitals, the right appearance, and other competitions, she can easily become an adult who believes she has to go out in the world and work for the love she craves. An even bigger challenge is that love perceived as conditional in childhood makes receiving the message of God's grace more difficult.

Because the perfect parent has yet to be created, a lot of grown children are busily working through life handicapped by a deficit of the love they most wanted and needed. To cope, they often resist the risks of the future and miss out on much of the joy God planned for them. With God, though, it is never too late! In the next chapters, we'll talk about how to improve your self-concept and increase your potential for joy. Keep reading!

A Prayer of Permission

Father God,

I praise you for my uniqueness. You have not put another person in the world who is just like me. Prepare me to

be the masterpiece that you originally created me to be.
Thank you for making me in your likeness. Allow me to
see myself today with as much significance as you see
me. Keep my focus ahead of me rather than behind me.
Protect me from overidentifying with my blunders and
underidentifying with my victories. Disrupt and dissolve
any stale, destructive self-talk from the past that I may
still be embracing.

Grant me the courage to push beyond previous boundaries **57**
in all areas of my life. Remind me that my peak moments
are just glimpses of the enormous potential you have
blessed me with. Thank you for giving me permission
to live life to the fullest!

In Jesus' name,

Amen

This One Thing I Do . . .

Beginning today, I increase my potential for
joy by meditating on what it truly means to be
a beautiful, wonderful child of God.

PART ONE SUMMARY

Discovering Your Joy

- Being joy filled does not mean that your life is perfect. It means that you emphatically trust God and believe that he has great plans for your life, regardless of what is happening right now. Joy is an outward sign of inward faith in the promises of God.
- Your thoughts are showing! Little by little, the secret conversations that you hold in the privacy of your own mind are determining your destiny.
- The 4:8 Principle states that whatever you give your attention to expands in your experience. If you dwell on your strengths, your blessings, your goals, and all the people who love you, then you will attract even more blessings, even more love, and even more accomplishments.
- The most effective technique for instilling the habit of 4:8 Thinking is developing the habit of repeatedly asking and answering 4:8 Questions. A 4:8 Question demands a positive, constructive response, which promotes 4:8 Thinking.
- We usually act consistently with our self-concept. You can override past negative programming by purposefully choosing behaviors that align with your full potential, regardless of whether or not you feel like it.

Think on These Things

The 4:8 Challenge

1. What do you believe is the secret to a joy-filled life?
2. In what ways have you been waiting for joy, instead of seeking it?
3. What kind of questions do you routinely ask yourself? How could better questions add to your joyful thinking?
4. How could you use the 4:8 Principle to bring out the best in your spouse? in your children?

PART TWO

POWER, LOVE, AND A SOUND MIND

Developing Your Joy

CHAPTER 4

YOUR POTENTIAL FOR JOY

Fortifying Your Self-Concept

Most players are pretty good, but they go to where the puck is.
I go to where the puck is going to be.
– Wayne Gretzky

In chapter 3, we talked about how a positive self-concept reflects our identity as God's children and enables us to reach our full potential. In this chapter, you will learn how to supercharge your potential for joy by building a godly self-concept. Here is a great opportunity! Regardless of where you are now or where you've been, you can take your self-concept to new heights by putting into practice any or all of the eight steps that follow. As you become familiar with these building blocks, I recommend that you evaluate how well you are already practicing each component. In the margin of this book, give yourself an old-fashioned letter grade. The intent of this quick exercise is not to make you feel inferior or superior, but to help you estimate where you are right now and determine what you could be doing to bolster your potential for joy. Remember, according to the 4:8 Principle, you will experience more of whatever you dwell on. If you meditate on your strengths, your God-given worth, and your future potential, you will be amazed at how differently you will view yourself.

Because your self-concept is your personal foundation for the future, every effort you make to fortify it will pay multiple rewards—and you will be well on your way to living a joy-filled life and having an even greater impact on the world.

Step one: Recognize the true source.

Legitimate, lasting self-worth can come only from God's love, from knowing and experiencing who you are as a new creation in Christ. See yourself as a child of God. You are God's special enterprise! Work to recognize that fact emotionally—not just intellectually. **If you keep thinking of yourself the way you used to be, that is exactly what you will continue to be.**

Too many people base their self-worth on what others think about them. But, if you depend on others for your self-worth, is it even accurate to call it *self*-worth? Beware of making a god of other people's opinion. Needing approval from others is an immobilizing trap. It is essentially saying that someone else's opinion of you is more important than God's. It may be helpful in certain situations to remind yourself quietly, "What you think of me is none of my business."

When you stay focused on God's promises, you realize that you have *already* been approved. Authentic self-worth is intrinsic. It comes from within, not from acquisitions, accolades, or approval from others. Despite your shortcomings, weaknesses, and blunders, God loves you. The Bible is full of this truth. One of many passages that express God's love is Jeremiah 31:3: "I have loved you, my people, with an everlasting love. With unfailing love I have drawn you to myself" (NLT).

Agree with your Creator! He knows everything about you, and he still loves you. Your love for yourself should mirror his love for you. This is critical, because you will receive only what, deep down, you believe you are worthy of having.

When you incorporate the 4:8 Principle into every corner of your life, you think, talk, and act as if you really believe you are this new creation. You act as if you sincerely believe old things have passed away and the Kingdom of God is within you. Consider what sort of self-image you are building with the flow of words, pictures, and images that race through your mind.

Step two: Forgive others without exception— and mean it!

You must forgive everyone in your life, past or present, for all the silly, spineless, nutty, nasty, gutless, cruel, spiteful, harmful, insensitive things they've ever done to you, both real and imagined. (Did I leave anything out?) As I mentioned in the last chapter, life is way too short to be negative.

> You cannot feel terrific about yourself when you feel poorly toward others.

We're all human. Stuff happens. Move on. **Never let an old wound fester due to excessive attention.** When you carry around bitterness, hostility, and other emotional baggage, you live in the past and cannot possibly realize your potential for joy. How does this affect your self-concept? It is impossible to feel terrific about yourself when you are lugging around resentment toward another person. I may be wrong, but I suspect this is by divine design.

Because no one is perfect, forgiveness will have to be an ongoing process. You must either develop an ultrathick skin or become a perpetual forgiveness machine—maybe even both. People, especially those closest to you, will continually hurt you, either intentionally or unintentionally. Frequently it will be in a small way; every now and then it will be in a supersized way. Make forgiveness a key component of what I call your *daily joy ritual*—a series of short steps you do routinely every morning or evening. Refuse to cling to hard feelings in any shape, form, or fashion. While you may be *forgiving others,* you are more directly *giving to yourself.* Your spiritual, emotional, mental, and physical health depends on your becoming a perpetual forgiveness machine.

Step three: Forgive yourself early and often— and mean it!

Now that you've made forgiving others a daily habit, add forgiving yourself to the list. In comparison, forgiving others might be easy! However, it's imperative to forgive yourself, without mental reservation, for your stupid choices, inappropriate thoughts, limiting words, foolish behaviors, negative beliefs, and all the other self-defeating things you've ever done. Because you are not perfect, forgiving yourself will be an ongoing process. Remarkably, you only have to do this . . . forever! That's okay; you're not alone.

Don't expect to *feel* any different instantly. The emotional blessing often lags behind the actual act of forgiveness. Just accept God's grace and restoration for the incredible gift that it is. Leave the junk behind so you can make room for the joy.

Practice forgiving yourself regularly—and mean it sincerely. Acknowledge your mistakes and accept God's forgiveness. After all, Jesus paid the price, so there is no reason for you to feel guilty beyond the point where you repent. If you look in the mirror and are ashamed by your reflection, you're sunk before you start. Instead of suffocating in past sin, bask in the tranquility and joy of spirit that flows through you when you realize that God has already pardoned you. Yesterday is in the history books. Yesterday is as unchangeable as World War II. Today, though, you are making history.

Guilt isn't practical. It forces you to experience the present moment while paralyzed by past mistakes. When you have setbacks or slip a bit, you aren't any less valuable. You simply have something to learn from slipping. Make sure you learn it, as learning from the past is much better than reliving it. Make forgiving yourself a mandatory element in your daily joy ritual. Forget your failures and relive your joys.

Step four: Focus on your God-given strengths.

Emphasize your originality by highlighting your special gifts and talents. No one else has your unique design, and God has a purpose for how he made you. This means there is no future in worshiping your weaknesses. Forget about your shortcomings and think about your God instead. With the gift of the Holy Spirit, you are qualified right now to do whatever God wants you to do. Surrender the idea that you need something or someone else to make you complete. As a child of God, you already have everything you need. You have what it takes. Lose yourself in serving others with your one-of-a-kind talent bank. Think about it: **If you were just like everyone else, what would you have to offer the world?** Instead of comparing yourself with others, which sooner or later becomes a downer, compete against your God-given potential. Become superior—to your previous self. Focus on unyielding self-development. Ask yourself repeatedly, "How am I better, stronger, and wiser today than I was yesterday?" Honor God by constantly raising your standards.

Often a poor self-concept is the result of comparing yourself unfavorably with someone else. I joke in my workshops that it would be almost impossible for you to have a negative self-concept if you were stranded on a desert island by yourself, because you wouldn't be able to compare yourself unfavorably with others. (Unless, of course, you blamed yourself for being stuck there!) Evaluate your progress in light of your full potential, not that of others. Don't ask, "How am I doing compared to them?" Ask instead, "How am I doing today compared with last quarter? How am I doing today versus where I was a year ago, or even yesterday?" Focus on improving yourself—you are the only person you can control.

Concentrate on progress, and give up the notion of perfection. Someone out there will always be better than you in at least one area of life. Similarly, you are going to be better than lots of other people at lots of things. We are superior to many folks in many ways, and we are inferior in many ways—and that is absolutely fine. Work on yourself.

Step five: Eliminate negative self-talk and introduce joy-talk.

Stop beating up on yourself—starting right now. Instead, speak to and about yourself as if you've already fulfilled your highest potential as defined in your personal mission statement. Unless you've laid out a gloomy vision for your future, this mechanism will put you in sync with the 4:8 Principle, because you'll be setting your mind on the praiseworthy aspects of your life. In light of God's best plans for you, what kind of words should you be using in your private conversations with yourself?

Changing the way you communicate with yourself changes your self-concept faster than any other single method. In Proverbs 18:21, we are advised that both life and death are in the power of the tongue. **The words you mutter to yourself have the power to encourage or discourage, to motivate or deflate, to generate joy or repel it.** When you use your mouth to argue for your limitations, you get to keep them. The words you use today will create the world you'll experience tomorrow. Depending on your focus, that is either a great problem or a great opportunity.

Imagine you've got a microphone hanging around your neck, and every word you speak today will be recorded and played back on national TV tomorrow. Would this be a good thing? Would your words accurately reflect your faith in God? Would your speech be more likely to represent the problems of the present or your hopes for the future? Would your words emphasize your blessings or your worries? Would you be pleased with your example to the world? Although you may not have an actual microphone, your words are being recorded in your subconscious and will be played back at a time of its choosing.

Become aware of your words. When someone asks how you are doing, how do you answer? Do you give the standard "fine" or "okay"? Why not use that everyday question as an opportunity to claim your joy? Reply, "I'm doing terrific!" or "Excellent, thanks!" or "I'm fantastic." Why? First of all, compared to millions if not billions of people in the world who struggle to meet the most basic needs, you *are* doing great. Second, your answer acts as a command to your subconscious. If you want an average day, then answer, "Fine, thanks." If you want something more, then avoid the boring, joy-resistant replies. Remember, joy is within you, but it is up to you to release it.

> It's not what goes into your mouth that defiles you; you are defiled by the words that come out of your mouth.
> — Matthew 15:11, NLT

Begin to **speak only what you seek,** as if you are already the person God intends for you to become and are already living the life of your dreams. Speak as if what is written in your mission statement is true today. Speak as if you believe in your prayers. Stop clinging to the past by talking about yourself as the person you no longer desire to be. Avoid making repeated, passing references to your mistakes and fears. First and foremost, cut out all self-deprecating remarks. I can develop a clear picture of someone's self-concept just by listening to them speak for fifteen or twenty minutes. They reveal it in the way they talk about themselves and frequently in the way they talk about others.

You can control what comes out of your mouth. Your words are, of course, a reflection of your thought process, but it is a bit easier to control your mouth than it is your mind. **Start programming your mind by first disciplining your mouth.** Cut out, one by one, every expression or remark that is inconsistent with the person God wants you to be.

71

Step six: Practice extreme self-care.

Get into and maintain excellent physical condition. Practicing *"extreme self-care,"* or caring meticulously for your mind, spirit, and body, is a natural by-product of a godly self concept. When you neglect the wise habits of good health, you make yourself much more vulnerable to the worst aspects of human nature. When you become drained, run down, or fatigued, you tend to violate the 4:8 Principle and get stuck in the negative. You may also make daily choices based on expediency—choices driven by a short-term payback rather than a long-term gain. Without maximum energy, you give less to the important people and causes in your life.

A high priority for my 1% Club clients is to maintain a brain and body that will help them function effectively, serve others, and follow through on their good intentions. **When you take exceptionally good care of yourself, you**

are much more likely to make decisions that will release your brakes and keep your tank full of joy. The alternative is to be so worn down that you just trudge along, allowing chains to keep you confined to something far less than who you really are.

Here are essential self-care factors to consider:

1. Am I living the life God intends for me?
2. Do I have a clear, compelling vision for my future?
3. Am I investing time alone each day with God?
4. Does anyone in my life hold me accountable to my best self?
5. Do I consistently make health-producing food and drink choices?
6. Am I exercising in some way almost every day?
7. Am I getting sufficient sleep most nights?
8. Do I have at least three close personal relationships?
9. Do I have *"extra time"* or *margin* built into my life-style?
10. Am I focused on progress rather than perfection?

Use your answers to help you pinpoint the areas where you need the most work. Develop a plan to get you where you want and need to be.

Step seven: Dwell on the person God wants you to become.

Using Philippians 4:8 as a trigger, visualize your best self. To accomplish this, first escape from the limitations of the current moment and shine your spotlight on your full potential.

After all, **there is much more to all of us than our current reality!** The majority of your true identity cannot be seen with human eyes. Your growth stalls when your invisible potential is not fed with attention and positive expectation. But before you can dwell on the person God wants you to become, you must define what you believe that is. As I mentioned in part one, I recommend that you develop a meticulously clear personal mission

> Stop judging by mere appearances, and make a right judgment.
> — John 7:24, NIV

statement that lays out your full potential in this lifetime as you believe God sees it. This is a vital point—not as you see it, but from God's point of view as best as you can determine it.

Listen to Paul's encouragement: "God can do anything, you know—far more than you could ever imagine or guess or request in your wildest dreams! He does it not by pushing us around but by working within us, his Spirit deeply and gently within us" (Ephesians 3:20, THE MESSAGE). In other words, broaden your horizon! Enlarge your mental territory. Use your imagination, not your memory, to achieve this faith-driven perspective. "The things which are impossible with men are possible with God" (Luke 18:27, NKJV). Craft your mission statement as if God himself were encouraging you in person.

You will find that this exercise forces you to stretch well beyond the status quo and bring out the best in yourself. Think of this view as your "spiritual eyes." We are, of course,

73

created in God's image and likeness. Consequently, we have an exciting and demanding responsibility. With *spiritual eyes*, we are able to see beyond the obvious surface appearance to the deeper spiritual realities.

All great leaders, spouses, parents, and coaches exercise these *eyes of faith*. They see potential and truth even though these concepts may be temporarily obscured in a veil of negativity. They acknowledge that the sun exists when only clouds are visible. They recognize great strength even in the midst of great struggles. They discern opportunities when others see only gridlock. Appearances, after all, can be quite deceiving. Spiritual eyes detect and draw out excellence in others.

After you write your personal mission statement, I want you to design a bold set of long- and short-term goals that awaken joy for the present and passion for the future. Finalize your God-inspired mission in writing, and compare your behavior and habits to it each week or even daily. Consider the possible ways your life could leave a lasting legacy. Then *dwell* on this written, consciously created version of your *self-ideal*. By *dwell* I mean reread it, rehearse it, memorize it, and envision it becoming your reality. Soak yourself in this ultimate vision. When you think deeply about the person you intend to become, you sensitize yourself to the changes you must

> Treat a man as he is and he will remain as he is. Treat a man as he could be and should be and he will become as he could be and should be.
> — Johann von Goethe

make to bring it about. Honor and acknowledge in others the qualities that you want to realize in your own life. Meditate frequently on the character qualities you believe God wants to see in you. The most joyful place you can be is in God's will. **Contemplate the wonderful and exciting plans God has in store for your future.**

One approach is to ask yourself, *"How would the future me respond to . . .* [name a specific situation]*? What would the future me do differently each morning or evening? How would the future me take care of my brain and body?"* Visualize the new you making better choices today and enjoying the rewards that naturally follow. Imagine yourself with the habits you would have if you were already living your best life.

Step eight: Act with joy now.

Anyone can be happy when circumstances are wonderful, but joy is different. Joy is proactive happiness. It is the learned capacity to display your faith ahead of time by means of your daily mental attitude. This should be one of the primary things separating men and women of faith from everyone else. Most people will just wait and see. A typical mind-set is, "When I see it, I'll believe it—and *then* I'll act on it." They've got it backward and will no doubt be doing a lot of waiting. Is the "show me first" approach indicative of a strong faith? No! The Bible gives us many examples of people who believed God's promises and let that shape their attitude—even when they couldn't yet see how God would act. Abraham and Sarah were elderly before God gave them a child, yet "by faith Abraham, even though he was past age—and Sarah herself was barren—was enabled to become a father because he considered him faithful who had made the promise" (Hebrews 11:11, NIV).

To act with joy now, live each hour as if your full potential has already materialized. Proceed, moment by moment, with the gratitude you'd have if your most heartfelt prayers have been answered. **Arise from your prayer time with a jubilant smile overtaking your face.** Essentially, this means exercising *spiritual eyes.* Look at your circumstances with the eyes of faith and see what *could be* if you would change your attitude and allow God to work in the situation.

I want you to stop reading briefly and make a list of five things you would be doing differently today if you had already reached your biggest goals or overcome your greatest challenges. Maybe you would be acting boldly, pursuing a passion, using your time differently, investing more time with important relationships, expressing thanks more often, or taking new risks. Why not go ahead and get the momentum going? Ask, "How would I act if I were bubbling with joy?"

At The 1% Club's annual couples' planning retreat, I often paraphrase Goethe's wisdom by saying, "Treat your wife as she is and she will remain as she is. Treat her as she could be and should be, and she will become as she could be and should be." As a parenting tool, we teach, "Treat your son as he could be and should be, and he will grow into what he could be and should be."

In marriage, you *can* become the type of partner who brings out the full potential in your relationship—*if you are willing to take the initiative.* Instead of being a reactive husband, you can think, speak, and act toward your wife like she is the woman of your dreams. You can choose to love her with joy *now*. Instead of being a reactive wife, waiting for obvious grounds for being loving, you can treat your husband like he is already exceeding your every expectation. You can choose to joyfully respect him *now*. Independent of what your mate does, *you* can honor the potential of your marriage.

Parents are often very good at exercising spiritual eyes with their kids. If you have kids (or remember being a kid), you can probably relate to this. Even when a baby is still only crawling, parents clearly envision the child eventually walking. Despite very little outward progress to suggest that he will ever walk, parents keep the faith. Stumble after stumble, bump after bump, they coach, encourage, and affirm him. Believing that he will indeed walk, *they respond to his potential*, not his current reality. A similar dynamic takes place years later when he is learning to read or to ride a bike. Often, though, as the child grows older, his parents set aside their spiritual eyes and become bogged down in the current reality. Still stumbling, only in different ways now, this child needs the potential-releasing power of spiritual eyes more than ever.

Imagine that someone offered you $75,000 to play the part of a joy-filled friend, wife, mom, or neighbor in a movie. Could you do it? Play that role now. When you behave the way you know you *would* behave if your prayer had been answered, then you are walking your walk, demonstrating your faith. Maybe you are not ready to do this in all areas of your life. That is okay for now, but don't let that justify inaction in the other areas. Take action now. You can do it!

The eight steps we've covered in this chapter provide you with tangible ways to improve your self-concept and incorporate the 4:8 Principle into the way you think. Some of these approaches are a bit unconventional, and they're not always a popular way to approach life, marriage, and parenting. I'd forgive you if you put this book down right now. But if you are still curious, then keep reading. You will be glad you did!

A Prayer for Self-Worth

Dear God,

Speak loudly to me and reveal all limiting images in my mind. Replace them with pictures that glorify you and accurately represent my full potential. Upgrade my opinion of myself and my vision for the future so I never feel the need to protect and preserve the past. Show me how to be a faithful steward of my one and only opportunity to magnify the greatness you have placed within me and to show your presence in my life. Lead me away from complacency and any temptation to settle for less than what you know is my absolute best.

How awesome it is that you know everything about me and love me anyway! As I accept and experience your grace and mercy, help me to grasp the depth and perfection of your love as demonstrated by the sacrifice of your only Son. Restore me this day, and make me whole and complete.

In Jesus' name,

Amen

This One Thing I Do . . .

Beginning today, I increase my potential for joy by forgiving myself and others without exception or mental reservation.

CHAPTER 5

YOU MAKE ME SO MAD!

Taking Charge of Your Emotional Life

If you are distressed by anything external, the pain is not due to the thing itself but to your own estimate of it; and this you have the power to revoke at any moment.

– Marcus Aurelius

My goal in writing this book is for you to experience nothing less than maximum joy! I believe that most people aim way too low in life and receive far less than God had in store for them. How about you? Are you fully alive and fully engaged with the opportunity to make the most of your one and only lifetime? Are you living each moment with the interest, wonder, and excitement of a young child? Life is meant to be a grand adventure for those few who dare to seize each day as if it were their last.

I want to push you to expect more from yourself and from life. This is your one shot, so why settle for anything less than joy? You have probably already discovered that I am a big fan of high standards. All lasting progress starts with a challenge to raise the bar, push the envelope, or otherwise cut a new, better path. And remember, the end goal—your joy—*blesses others.* When putting the 4:8 Principle in practice and living with joy, you focus on the potential in others rather than their flaws—so you treat them with more patience and kindness. And when you're truly joy filled, others are inspired to find that source of joy themselves. Your joy blesses your spouse. Your joy blesses your children. Your joy blesses your friends. Your joy blesses even your adversaries. Your joy blesses all humanity. And your joy will leave a legacy that affects generations to come. Your Father in heaven is a God of laughter and joyfulness and gladness. With that in mind, what does a mediocre attitude transmit to the world and reveal about your faith? How could a bored, sullen, or defeatist attitude ever glorify him?

How are you doing in this area? Do you radiate unmistakable joy that has but one source? Can you imagine any greater way to draw others to Christ than through your nonstop expression of joy? Could there be a more attractive light than uncontainable joy? I challenge you to look at each day as an unrepeatable opportunity to express the light of your full potential to the world.

With that as the goal, in this chapter we'll discuss one of the most significant barriers to experiencing joy: not taking charge of your emotional life, or having a victim mentality regarding emotions. When was the last time you heard someone say, "You make me so mad!"? I used that line as a title for this chapter because it is a common phrase that particularly exemplifies a disempowering emotional life. Of course, there are many variations of this phrase. You can fill in the blank or substitute words, but whenever you transfer the ownership of your emotional life to someone else, you are losing power over your emotions. You are losing emotional strength. In this chapter and the next, I will equip you with some practical methods for mastering your emotional life and producing more joy. As you become familiar with these concepts, keep in mind that progress, not perfection, is the objective. Put the thought of perfection out of your mind, and emphasize daily improvement instead.

Building Emotional Strength

In the pages that follow, I want to prepare you to build your emotional strength so that you can overcome the negative feelings that deplete your energy and minimize your potential for joy. Emotional strength refers to three things:

- Emotional resiliency
- Emotional control
- Emotional toughness

Emotional strength fuels your capacity to experience the fullness of life without the disruption of prolonged bouts of negativity. Gray attitudes become the exception, not the expectation. With emotional strength, down moments are viewed in the light of truth and acknowledged for what they really are. Emotional strength is not about denying your problems. It is about acknowledging a far greater power—**affirming God rather than affirming your woes.** The foundation of emotional strength is mental well-being. When you focus your thoughts on what is noble and right, as in the 4:8 Principle, you develop your mental muscle. Without this mental muscle, you will inevitably experience cracks in your "foundation" that will frustrate your efforts at living a joy-filled life. And this path to emotional strength

83

begins with a change of focus. When you change your focus, you change your emotional life.

Perception Is Reality—or Is It?

Emotions are subjective indicators of objective experience. For example, if you are hiking through the woods and you come across what you believe to be a snake in the path ahead of you, you will respond emotionally to that belief. You may experience fear and stop in your tracks or quickly retreat. Whatever your response, it's rooted in how you interpret what you're observing with your senses.

> It is not enough to have a good mind. The main thing is to use it well.
> — René Descartes

Imagine that as you step back, you look a little more closely and realize that the "snake" is in fact only a rope lying in the path. You interpreted it as a snake, and then your emotions, followed by your body, reacted to what you *thought* you saw. It didn't matter that the rope lying in the path was no threat at all. Perception was reality. You believed it to be true. You misinterpreted the rope as being dangerous, and you automatically reacted consistently with that perception.

It is easy to do this in all sorts of situations, especially with the important people in your life. For example, it is quite common for spouses to express irritation with the exact qualities in their mate that seemed so attractive while they were dating. Sometimes it takes a very good and diplomatic friend to point out that the reality has not changed—only the perception. Have you ever experienced this? Remember, **when your interpretations change, your emotions change.** That means you are not a victim of your emotions; you can shape them by the way you choose to think. Your job is to keep the emotional spiral pointing upward. Your task is to become proficient at interpreting the events of your life in such a way that you remain empowered to improve them.

Once when I was about twelve years old, my family's burglar alarm went off around midnight. I was at home with one of my older sisters when the siren began screaming. Startled, we presumed it was a false alarm for thirty seconds or so, until the system's control panel, by infrared beams positioned in our hallways, indicated that an intruder was moving through the house. Even though we knew the police were on the way, we were terrified. At one point, we were both hunched down near a side door trying to decide whether to stay in the house or make a run for it. With the siren still going and our hearts racing, I suddenly realized something significant: We had mistakenly set the alarm in "away" mode, which is the setting for when no one will be at home. I remember standing up not so boldly, silencing the siren, and explaining to my sister what I thought had happened: She had walked down the stairs on the way to the kitchen and had been detected by the interior beam. As I rushed through the house to find her, I too was detected. *We* were the "intruders" moving through the house. We had incorrectly programmed the burglar alarm, causing it to go off for no valid reason.

Again, this is very easy for us to do with our emotional life. We can inadvertently program ourselves to react a certain way, even if that reaction is not based on reality.

When you acknowledge that your emotions are not necessarily based on truth, *that recognition alone* will downsize the damage that a negative emotion can trigger. Our emotions cannot be totally trusted, nor can they be denied outright. They should not be worshiped, but neither should they be ignored. Think of emotions as biochemical couriers that provide feedback on your current mood. Emotions allow you to feel what you are thinking at this particular moment. They are the vehicle through which joy or pain is communicated. Negative emotions reveal that your mental health is suffering, just as physical pain shows that your body is suffering.

Emotions are a set of interconnected thoughts that have been intensified through repetition. A thought, positive or negative, that races through your mind without much feeling doesn't have much effect on your body or your behavior. Those fleeting thoughts don't stop you, pull you down, or throw you offtrack. But intensified thoughts can do all of these things. That's why it's very wise to keep them under control.

Because you can control your thoughts, you can strengthen your emotional life. Most people have enormous room for improvement in this area.

What Are Your Emotional Goals?

Has anyone ever asked you about your goals? You've probably been asked about your financial goals, your fitness goals, your spiritual goals, and maybe even your family goals. But have you ever been asked about your *emotional goals*? These should not be left to chance. You cannot afford to wing it when it comes to your emotional well-being. Give your brain a specific intention, and it will serve you well. Feed your brain mixed messages, and it will hold you back.

Because you're reading this book, I assume you are interested in more joy. What are some of the other positive emotions you'd like to experience more often? If you could wave a magic wand and improve your emotional life in any specific way, how would you choose to improve it? Knowing these answers is what I mean when I suggest "emotional goals." What are the emotions you want to experience more often and more intensely? Which ones do you want to experience less frequently or with less intensity? Use the following two lists, or *emotional menus,* to help you clarify your goals:

87

ON THE NEGATIVE SIDE

- Fear
- Resentment
- Boredom
- Loneliness
- Fatigue
- Insecurity
- Guilt
- Depression
- Rage
- Overload
- Confusion
- Exhaustion

ON THE POSITIVE SIDE

- Joy
- Excitement
- Contentment
- Confidence
- Peace
- Passion
- Drive
- Satisfaction
- Enthusiasm
- Awe
- Energy
- Gratitude

Circle the top three emotions you would like to experience more often over the next thirty days. If your target emotions did not appear on the above list, write in your own. Then transfer your answers to the front of a three-by-five card under the heading "Increase!" Next, choose three emotions you would like to experience less often, and transfer them to the back of the same card under the heading "Decrease!"

The joy of the LORD is your strength.
— Nehemiah 8:10, NIV

I want you to use this card as your bookmark for the remainder of this book so that you will stay mindful of your intentions. As you work through the upcoming chapters, you can apply what you are reading to your specific emotional goals. In fact, you cannot separate a discussion of emotional strength from a discussion of mental discipline. In the next segment of this chapter, you will learn three dynamic and practical laws to help you steer your emotional life in the direction you desire.

A 30 Percent Improvement

Let me ask you some odd questions. (I know they are odd because of the unusual facial expressions I have observed when I've asked them in private coaching sessions.) **What would have to happen for you to get 30 percent better at managing your emotional life? How could that improvement influence the rest of your life? How could it affect your health, your marriage, your parenting, or your career?**

I am not suggesting a 50 or 100 percent improvement. My challenge to you, in this chapter and the next, is to start taking steps to improve the quality of your emotional life by 30 percent. I know that this will be impossible to measure precisely, but it supplies you with an achievable vision for improving your emotions. It is a helpful mental construct because it reassures you that progress—not perfection—is the priority. Thirty percent seems significant yet achievable over a reasonable period of time. I'll leave the time frame up to you, but make sure to set a deadline for re-evaluating your progress.

I've taught the clear-cut approach you are about to learn for many years in my coaching practice. I have consistently received positive reports such as these:

- "At first I thought everyone else had changed. Then I realized *I* had changed."

- "I finally recognized my role in this situation."
- "The man I married has returned."

Imagine for a moment the difference an emotional break-through could make in the quality of your relationships and in your quest for joy. Will it be worth the effort? I think you already know the answer.

You can control your thoughts; therefore, you can significantly improve your emotional strength, including, of course, your potential for joy. Our feelings seldom provide reliable advice for decision making. Much of the world would have you believe otherwise. Popular culture encourages us to follow our feelings, even though emotions can swiftly cloud our ability to make wise decisions or choices that we will be proud of when all is said and done. Hardly a week passes without the headline of another celebrity breakup, usually with a publicist announcing, "They *felt* it was time to move on," "They lost *feelings* for each other," or something similar.

90

> Visible circumstances are the result of invisible thoughts.

Unfortunately, the rest of the population is not far behind. Well-meaning husbands and wives withhold the love and respect they unconditionally pledged because they no longer *feel* like delivering it. Teenagers and young adults *feel* their way into decisions that will shape their future indefinitely. Business leaders *feel* their way into corrupt endeavors that scar them, their organizations, and their families for years to come. It doesn't have to be this way. Are we as a society chasing joy in all the wrong places? Remember that although feelings fluctuate, consequences last forever.

The Laws of Emotional Strength

To master your emotional life, you must understand three simple maxims that concisely explain the mental dynamics of emotional health. When you operate in harmony with these laws, you naturally produce a satisfying emotional climate. You cannot evade detection when you violate these principles (as you can with manmade laws), even though the consequences may take months or even years to surface. These interconnected laws are continuously influencing your character, your personality, and your potential for joy, whether you realize it or not. You will find these laws easy to identify with and to turn to your advantage when you decide to do so.

The Law of Attention

This is the 4:8 Principle in a nutshell: *Whatever you dwell upon becomes increasingly prominent in your own mind.* For example, the more you emphasize your good health with both your silent thoughts and public speech, the healthier you feel. The more you stay mindful of the positive qualities in your spouse, the closer and stronger your relationship will become. The more attention you give your kids, the more influence you will have in their lives. The more you mull over God's promises, the greater your spiritual convictions become. Alternatively, the more you mentally replay a particular injustice, the more frustrated you will,

91

without a doubt, become. Your emotional life can advance only after your negative thoughts retreat. **You will always feel what you dwell on.**

If your emotional life today is not where you ultimately want it to be, then your top priority should be shifting your attention to your blessings, to your strengths, and to the aspects of your life that are working. Resist the urge to accelerate negative emotional spirals by chronically reporting your own negative headlines. Stop talking so much about your mistakes, setbacks, and disappointments. Refuse to fuel negative emotions by constantly talking about what is wrong with your marriage, your oldest kid, your sore back, your strange neighbors, and the world in general. Instead, broadcast your blessings to anyone who will listen. Verbalize your vision for the future to trusted friends and allies. Turn the spotlight of your concentration to your future hopes and dreams, to the grand and mysterious future that God has in store for you.

Think about watching the evening news. Even though lots of great, positive things are going on in the world, almost everything the television news highlights is terrible stuff that has, unfortunately, already happened. Arguably, there is not a lot to gain from watching it, unless it prompts you to take productive action or deepens your understanding of important events. But it is definitely worth evaluating the current quantity of bad news that you ingest. Even the weather reports slant toward the negative. Imagine hearing "There's a 70 percent chance of sunshine tomorrow" instead of "There's a 30 percent chance of rain." You'd fall off the couch! Leading with the negative is how the news is delivered, but it doesn't have to be how you run your life. Even though there will always be cloudy days, you don't have to make blemishes the essence of your life. Leave that for the news reporters. That is their job, not yours.

The flip side of the Law of Attention is that whatever you stop thinking about or turn your attention away from tends to atrophy and drop out of your life. Starve worry, fear, and doubt by no longer nourishing them with your attention. Remember, whatever you focus on, you are going to experience. If you have an urge to "go negative," remember that it's not going to produce anything positive.

93

The Law of Exchange

This simply means that **you can do away with a negative thought only when you replace it with a positive thought.** If you like, you can also purge positive thoughts by substituting them with negative thoughts. I don't know why anyone would want to do that, but that option, as you've probably observed, seems to be widely practiced. Your conscious mind can hold only one thought at a time, and that one thought is either in alignment with your potential for joy or it is not. This is good news because it means you can swap an average thought with a brilliant thought or a fearful thought with a courageous thought whenever you choose.

Let me tell you what does *not* work: You cannot eliminate a thought by fighting it or trying to block it out. Resisting an unwanted thought only entangles you and drives that thought deeper into your mind, making it even more of a distraction. If you are upset with your spouse and try to tell yourself not to be upset, you stay tuned in to what is aggravating you, and your mood stays down or even worsens. Here's another example: If we're playing golf and I say to you, "Don't think about hitting your ball into the trap," of course you immediately think of doing so. If you say, "I will not hit my ball into the trap," you're still thinking about it, because your brain finds it very difficult to concentrate on the reverse of something. The solution is to shift your attention to something else completely. When you switch to a higher channel mentally, you replace the previous, lower channel.

94

You can exert far greater control over your thinking and your life by replacing negative, counterproductive thoughts with positive, empowering thoughts. Thoughts of sand traps and hazards are replaced with precise thoughts about where you want your ball to land on the green. Thoughts of discontent with your spouse are displaced with thoughts of appreciation for the overall relationship or advance gratitude for the great future God surely has planned for both of you. Thoughts of boldness replace thoughts of doubt. Thoughts of winning dislodge thoughts of losing. **Productive thinking disrupts unproductive thinking.** You overcome evil with good. And when you preoccupy your mind with God's Word, you go a long way toward shutting out temptation. Here are some verses, in addition to Philippians 4:8, that are especially helpful in raising your state of mind.

God is our refuge and strength, an ever-present help in trouble. (Psalm 46:1, NIV)

You guide me with your counsel, leading me to a glorious destiny. (Psalm 73:24, NLT)

Trust in the LORD with all your heart and lean not on your own understanding; in all your ways acknowledge him, and he will make your paths straight. (Proverbs 3:5-6, NIV)

You will keep in perfect peace all who trust in you, all whose thoughts are fixed on you! (Isaiah 26:3, NLT)

Jesus said, "Come to me, all of you who are weary and carry heavy burdens, and I will give you rest." (Matthew 11:28, NLT)

The Kingdom of God is already among you. (Luke 17:21, NLT)

You will know the truth, and the truth will set you free. (John 8:32, NLT)

The thief comes only to steal and kill and destroy; I have come that they may have life, and have it to the full. (John 10:10, NIV)

I am leaving you with a gift—peace of mind and heart. And the peace I give is a gift the world cannot give. So don't be troubled or afraid. (John 14:27, NLT)

Forgetting the past and looking forward to what lies ahead, I press on to reach the end of the race and receive the heavenly prize for which God, through Christ Jesus, is calling us. (Philippians 3:13-14, NLT)

I can do everything through Christ, who gives me strength. (Philippians 4:13, NLT)

God has not given us a spirit of fear and timidity, but of power, love, and self-discipline. (2 Timothy 1:7, NLT)

Release the need to hang on to thoughts that haven't worked well in your life. If you want to gain emotional control, you first have to gain mental control. With the 4:8 Principle, this mental habit becomes second nature.

The Law of Reversibility

This simply refers to your God-installed capability to produce feelings as a result of deliberate behavior. **One of the most effective and least utilized methods for upgrading your emotional life is acting your way into the feelings you most desire.** If you're not experiencing as much joy, passion, or satisfaction as you would like, you can, over time, act your way into those higher emotions by behaving and thinking in ways consistent with your emotional goal. Most people resist this option because they have been conditioned to believe that positive emotions should happen naturally. Some people reason that if you have to work at it, it is not genuine. If it is authentic, it should be automatic, right? A handful of my students have even told me they felt like they were being phony or lying to themselves when they acted better than they actually felt at the moment.

I can understand these reactions, but one thing is certain: **If you rule out the option of acting into your feelings, you will forever be doomed to enjoy only those positive emotions that arise spontaneously.**

However, once you've decided that following Scripture and fulfilling your full potential dictates a particular choice, then "acting your way into feelings" is simply the discipline that will align your behavior with your values. God has built this power for personal change into all of us, even though it may not feel comfortable right away. Think about it. Any new behavior feels a bit unnatural until we grow accustomed to it. Even wearing a new pair of shoes requires a break-in period before they feel natural.

To those who feel as if they're lying when they act better than they feel, let me say that there is a far greater likelihood that their negative emotions, not their positive ones, are rooted in untruth. We'll talk about this more in the next chapter.

Let me illustrate the law of reversibility. Think of a time when you initially didn't feel like doing something. Most people can relate to occasionally waking up and feeling pretty lousy. However, within nine or ten minutes of being up and about, they feel absolutely fine, even without caffeine. This is the law in action. As another example, almost everyone has experienced the intention to exercise without an accompanying feeling of enthusiasm. I know I have! I've learned to push through this wall by getting myself moving. Just changing into my workout clothes keeps the momentum going. Then warming up moves me a little closer to the feeling I'm after. Once I'm on the treadmill or StairMaster, I almost feel like exercising. And within ten or fifteen minutes, I am embarrassed that I came so close to blowing off my workout. I force myself to act in a manner consistent with my values, not in a manner consistent with my feelings at that particular moment.

I remember leaving the office a few years ago and receiving a call on my mobile phone from my wife, who wanted me to run some errands on the way home. After I explained how tired I was, she reluctantly let me off the hook, and I headed toward home. A couple of minutes later, I received another call from a friend who was inviting me to join him last minute in front-row seats at the Atlanta Thrashers hockey game. Suddenly I had plenty of energy. But how would I explain this to Kristin? I mention this example because it demonstrates that our capacity to act into a feeling is restricted *only* by our motivation for doing so. I reinforced my feeling of fatigue when I focused on the hassle of the errands, yet seconds later, I instantly zapped the feeling of fatigue with the vision of the hockey game.

> The lamp of the body is the eye. Therefore, when your eye is good, your whole body also is full of light. But when your eye is bad, your body also is full of darkness.
> – Luke 11:34, NKJV

When you have a compelling reason, you can reach your emotional goals. You can sit around and wait for those feelings to be triggered from the outside, or you can behave your way into those blessings now. Even the word *emotion* itself is 86 percent *motion*. Take another look and you'll spot the secret of reversibility.

When you behave in a way that's pleasing to God, you will be rewarded with the emotional fruits you desire. When you experience a certain emotion, you can ask yourself sev-

98

eral questions: *Does this serve my vision and God-given potential? Does this emotion reflect reality or lazy thinking? Could it be the result of fatigue, a stray mood, or some unknown reason? Is this a goal-directed or a goal-deluding emotion? Does the feeling I'm having move me toward my full potential for joy and success, or in another direction?*

It's a definite leap of faith to act in a manner consistent with what you want to feel, but consider the alternative! Recognizing the Law of Attention, the Law of Exchange, and the Law of Reversibility is a great first step on your journey to emotional strength and well-being.

99

To end this chapter and get you prepared for the next one, I want you to imagine a pot of water boiling on the stove. Think of the boiling water as your negative emotions. If you dump a bunch of ice in the boiling water, it will stop boiling—but only temporarily, because the source of heat has not been addressed. In this illustration, the source of heat is erroneous thought patterns that have become automatic over time. To stop negativity and upgrade your potential for joy, you must either have lots of "ice" or correct the negative thinking. The ice may take different forms: excessive food, television, or alcohol; drugs; chronic busyness; or physical escapes. All these chill the water momentarily but do nothing to eliminate the cause of the heat. Even when you "let off steam" by removing the lid, you are only keeping the water from boiling over and making a mess.

In the next chapter, you are going to look underneath that pot and encounter the source. I suspect you already know what it will be. Here's a hint: I will not prompt you to exhume the past or resolve issues from your childhood. Instead, I am going to equip you to deal with your emotions *today* so that you can reap more joy *tomorrow*.

A Prayer for Emotional Strength

Father,

Thank you for the adventure of my life and for being with me every step along the way. Keep my mind from dwelling on what's wrong with people and situations, and instead, help me to focus on what's right, excellent, and worthy of praise. Show me how to affirm your power so that I don't think negatively about my problems. Inspire me to interpret the conditions I face in such a way that I remain constantly empowered to improve them.

I praise you for giving me dominion over my thought life and consequently over the quality of my emotions. Protect me from acting on feelings that are inconsistent with your Word. I know that obedience to your principles is the only true path to emotional health, vitality, and abundant joy. Just as figs do not come from thornbushes, I know that positive circumstances do not come from negative thoughts.

Teach me how to act in a manner consistent with uncontainable joy. Grant me the courage to act the way I would act if you were physically in my presence encouraging me. Thank you!

In Jesus' name,

Amen

This One Thing I Do . . .

Beginning today, I increase my potential for joy by starving worry, fear, and doubt, no longer nourishing them with my attention and conversation.

CHAPTER 6

HEAD GAMES

Starving Negative Emotions

It's not a lie if you believe it.
– George Costanza from *Seinfeld*

A classic fable begins with a grandfather telling his grandson about the two wolves battling inside his heart. "One is wise and kind, and the other is vicious and cruel," says the grandfather. "Which one will win?" asks the grandson. And the grandfather replies, "The one I feed."

In the previous chapter, we discussed how taking responsibility for our emotional life can increase our potential for joy. When our thinking is healthy and positive, our emotions will follow. In this chapter, I will discuss the common ways we feed negative emotions and some uncommon strategies for starving them.

An Animal in the Woods

We think in one of two primary ways. The most common is in reaction to the world around us, similar to how an animal in the woods reacts to a noise or to a threat of danger.

Often, we simply react to something that someone else does or says or to an experience we may have. We react with a particular thought that, if it persists, will generate an emotion, followed by an action consistent with that feeling. We move from thought to emotion to action. If we interpret the situation negatively, the resulting emotion is likely to be self-defeating. The behavior will probably move us away from what we really want, even though it may feel right and defensible at the moment. These emotional reflexes quickly become habits of mind.

The other way we can trigger thoughts is intentionally. We can create a *"to-think" list* such as Paul provides in Philippians 4:8, or we can simply borrow his. We can decide that lovely, gracious, pure, and excellent thoughts are constructive and the kind we want to think on a regular basis. Deliberately choosing 4:8 Thoughts produces the emotional life we want. They will stimulate good moods, and these moods will spur action consistent with the goals and ideals most important to us.

You can create a *virtuous cycle* like this by getting really clear on your personal vision and aligning your behavior with that vision, thereby producing the emotional blessings you desire. The alternative is to surrender your emotional life to the events of the day and live in constant suspense, acting consistently with your ideals only when you *feel* like it. Understand that your emotional strength is directly linked to your moral decisions. The choices you make that violate biblical truth invite emotional discord even though they may initially produce counterfeit joy. This emotional debt must always be paid back, with interest. But when you behave in

104

ways that are pleasing to God, you will be rewarded with the emotional fruit that your soul truly desires. When you live purposefully, think rightly, serve generously, and forgive quickly, you are laying the groundwork for emotional victory. I have found it very empowering to remind myself repeatedly that negative emotions are not God's will for my life.

I can offer specific strategies for dealing with negative emotions so that you move closer to a joy-filled life. As your coach, my goal is to help you reach this goal. But first, you have to come to grips with this fundamental question: *If it comes down to choosing between reaching your full potential or experiencing the negative emotion you believe you deserve, what's it going to be?*

We have all been in situations where we've almost enjoyed wallowing in negative emotions. We carry on angrily about the driver who cut us off long after he has disappeared from view; we nurse a grudge against someone who said something hurtful; or we sulk in response to being disappointed. But what is the end result? Will entertaining and acting on the negative emotion move us in the direction of our highest good? Will that negative emotion bless those closest to us? Will it help us reach our goals? In a marriage squabble, for example, is the goal to be right or to be happy?

What's your goal?

I bombard my clients with this question for the sole purpose of enhancing their spontaneous decision making. Your goal should act as a filter, eliminating words, behaviors, and other emotional responses that oppose it. As a parent, for example, your emotional responses can be tempered by a clearly stated parenting goal, such as communicating love, not impatience to your children, that weeds out irresponsible parental reactions regardless of their apparent justification. Certainly, you will have negative triggers in your life from time to time. Fortunately, just for his dearest creation, God has provided a little gap of opportunity. This tiny space between the stimuli and your response to it gives you a chance to think before you react. This will shape not only your potential for joy, but also your destiny as a human being.

106

Head Games

We do all sorts of silly things that fuel our negative emotions. As a result, we end up getting more of *what we don't want*. We distort things, we exaggerate things, we amplify our experiences in life, and then we pick the wrong things to dwell on. Philippians 4:8 clearly communicates *what we should do:* "Dwell on the things that are uplifting. Dwell on the things that are working. Dwell on the things that are worthy of praise." But frequently, we dwell on just the opposite of what Paul was referring to in this exceedingly practical passage from the New Testament. When you find yourself emotionally low, you can be pretty sure that you've been dwelling on what's not working. In this low state, your mind plays tricks on you. If you're trying to implement the 4:8 Principle, it is very important to start noticing your emotions and how they spiral quickly upward or downward. This peaked awareness shifts you from being the passenger in your emotional life to being the driver. Only when you notice changes in your emotional life can you begin to rise above the passive choices that fuel negative emotions.

Some negative thoughts stand out more than others. These "really awful thoughts," or RATs for short, terrorize your potential for joy. In this section, I will teach you how to spot them so that you can have a counterattack plan ready. The purpose of discussing these RATs is to pique your awareness, which will weaken the grip of negativity. After identifying the most common RATs, I will show you how to disrupt, dispute, and then deflect them. Keep in mind that these RATs highlight crooked *thinking patterns*, not crooked people. See if you can relate to any of the patterns described below.

Amplifiers magnify unpleasant situations with recurrent use of extreme words like *always, never, no one,* and *every time.* Virtually nothing in life falls in that excessive category. Frequently, these amplifiers show up in marriage and parenting. Aside from being distortions, these statements cause everyone involved to plummet below the joy zone.

Feelers accept negative feelings as true without questioning them. Sometimes your negative emotions reveal a deficiency in yourself or someone else, and sometimes they don't. Often what you feel is a simple distortion. Sometimes it is not objective, and it reflects the quality of your thinking more than it does the quality of your life experience. Though feelings are important, they are no substitute for the truth!

Guessers pretend they know what other people are thinking, and then they assume the worst ahead of time. This often triggers an emotional response from the other person, which in turn gets you defensive. This kicks off a cycle that is not very joyful.

Exaggerators transform mole hills into mountains with trigger words like *horrible, worst, ruined, shocked, devastated, stunned,* and *outraged.* I like to think of this as "Awfulizing" or "Drama Queen Syndrome."

Identifiers inject harmless events with personal meaning. They overestimate how the event is related to them. They take things too personally and interpret negative events as personal attacks. For example, if I get cut off in traffic and spill coffee in my lap, I might respond as if the other driver had been out to get me. Momentarily, I act as if I believe the other driver had carefully plotted to be at just that spot on the interstate, at just the right angle to cut me off. Once he identified my car, he thought, *"Ah, that's Tommy. Get him,"* and then drove right in front of me on purpose. We've all been irritated in a situation like that, haven't we?

Forecasters predict the worst-case scenario, often aloud and usually before they even get started participating in an activity, solving a problem, or engaging in an important conversation.

Cynics have a knack for finding something wrong, even if it is the *only* thing wrong. Despite the good, they use their mental radar to see the bad. Because there's always going to be some degree of bad stuff, cynics will forever be able to justify their viewpoint. Their reward is that they get to be more miserable. At The 1% Club's couples retreat, we put it like this: Your spouse has ten positive qualities and ten not-so-positive qualities, *and so do you.* But your experience of your mate will depend on which qualities you focus on most of the time.

Blamers point the finger at someone else for their own problems, even though it's rare that problems are caused entirely by someone else. As the opposite of responsibility, blame is so popular because it temporarily liberates you. It gives you a short-term emotional fix; you feel better for the time being. However, blaming others is ultimately immobilizing. It holds you back and cuts the legs right out from under your full potential for joy. Blame is like an emotional dirty bomb.

109

Justifiers remind themselves of all the reasons why they are entitled to this negative emotion or that negative outburst. Losing sight of their vision, justifiers are advocates for their own negativity. It manifests in language like "If you only knew what he did" or "I deserve to be upset."

Not exactly the stuff that joy is made of, is it? Now that you are aware of these RATs, I'll show you how to exterminate them and put an end to the games they orchestrate in your mind.

Starving Negative Emotions

When you deal with negative emotions, you have a couple of basic choices: You can suppress them by keeping them buried inside, ultimately making yourself sick. Or you can express your negativity to those closest to you (closest either in proximity or in relationship) and make them "sick" in the short term. Many people think those are the only two options. In other words, for most of the people you know, *suppression and expression are the only tools in the emotional toolbox.* As the old proverb goes, "If the only tool you have is a hammer, then everything starts to look like a nail." Is there any other way to effectively manage negative emotions? Are any other tools available? The answer is a resounding *yes!*

To live a life of *maximum* joy, you must learn how to *minimize* negative emotions so they will not dominate your life. Imagine covering a small campfire with a bucketful of dirt. Instantly it is snuffed out. Now think about your mindset prior to smothering it. First, you developed the desire to put out the fire, probably because you were leaving the campground or going to sleep. Then you made the decision to do so. Finally, you took action. If your goal was to put out the fire, you would never think of throwing on another log or dousing it with gasoline.

Negative emotions function in some ways like the campfire. How do you "put them out"? You extinguish them with positive, constructive thinking. You refuse to nourish them with the kind of attention that causes them to erupt into a blazing inferno. Alternatively, you can get out the gas can, dump it on your thought life, and aggravate the situation with inflammatory mental habits, emotional outbursts, and unwise decisions. But why in the world would you want to do that? If you have the desire to starve negative emotions, and you have made the decision to do it, here's what you *can* do:

1. You can acknowledge your negative emotions. God doesn't want you to be in constant emotional pain any more than he wants you to be in constant physical pain. Your natural state, both physically and emotionally, is one of health, harmony, and balance. Physical pain indicates that an injury or imbalance needs to be addressed. Typically, when you experience pain, you acknowledge these bodily signals and take action to correct them. You would never think of continuing to sprint around the track if your knee was swollen with fluid. However, on the emotional side, you often ignore similar signs and continue thinking and behaving as before.

It is helpful to think of a negative emotion as a warning light on your car's dashboard. If you ignore the indicator light, you may very well be inviting a bigger problem down the road. If you don't deal with it, the warning remains front and center wherever you go. Once you acknowledge it by taking your car in to get checked out, you can discover whether it's a real problem or a false alarm. Any necessary maintenance can be performed, and the caution light will disappear. In the same way, you can defuse your negative emotions by acknowledging their presence. Determine whether any critical needs are going unmet or whether this is just a false alarm.

2. You can put negative emotions in their place. One way to do this is to challenge their authenticity. When you become aware of a negative emotion, simply remind yourself, "This is just the way I feel. It's not necessarily the truth. It doesn't need to dictate my behavior." Feelings are not the gospel and are rarely cited in Scripture as a basis for taking action. Left unchecked, your feelings tend to drag you into the worst aspects of human nature, namely, shifting your attention and outlook from the long term to the short term. Instead of allowing your feelings to guide your decisions, allow God's Word to be your compass. Compliance with God's principles is the seldom discussed, timeless secret to sustained positive emotions. If you are held captive to how the world wants you to feel and behave, you must also endure the roller coaster of negative emotions that correspond with that philosophy. Put them in their place so that you realize they are not the basis for your decisions.

> We demolish arguments and every pretension that sets itself up against the knowledge of God, and we take captive every thought to make it obedient to Christ.
> – 2 Corinthians 10:5, NIV

112

3. You can own negative emotions. Declare, "I am responsible." The good news is that you don't even have to believe this completely. Affirming "I am responsible," even if you have to grit your teeth to do it, deflates negative emotions via the Law of Exchange. (You can do away with a negative thought only by replacing it with a positive thought.) The three words *I am responsible* pierce the illusion of blame and withhold the emotional oxygen it needs to survive. Accepting responsibility means you are responding maturely, in a way that keeps you more effective and creative. In this productive frame of mind, you are capable of seeing situations and solutions much more clearly. Beware: This is so simple that many people refuse to give it a try. But I encourage you to do it. Even if you can't stomach accepting any responsibility for the situation you find yourself in, you are still responsible for what you do about it. You are responsible for your reaction and whether it improves or worsens your circumstances.

The moment you stop blaming others, you're on the road to greater emotional health. When something goes wrong in your world, you must resist the temptation to extend that pointer finger in any other direction than back at yourself. The common tendency in our society is to blame events for causing us to feel and act the way we do. Whenever you catch yourself going down that tired path, activate the Law of Exchange and say to yourself, *"I am responsible."* The first few times you say it, it may not *feel* true. Stick with it and repeat it, because you know that it is the spiritual truth.

Relax—you're not accepting legal liability for negative situations. You are not proclaiming that another person didn't contribute to the problem. What you are doing is refusing to be brought down to a lower level because of what someone else does. Do not let another person determine your frame of mind. Life is too short for that. When you think or say the words *I am responsible,* they block other negative phrases from invading your mind and taking control of your disposition. The next time you start to feel negative, repeat those gut-wrenching words. Say them to yourself. *I am responsible.* Say them aloud, if possible. Very quickly, those negative, joy-suppressing thoughts will not feel welcome in your mental house. They will go and find somebody else who will coddle them.

4. You can starve negative emotions by tuning in to the big picture. Step back a bit and remind yourself of what's truly important. A change in perspective can quickly create a change in heart. If I had the opportunity

113

to meet with you as your coach, I would ask you these questions:

- What is your goal here?
- What outcome do you want in this situation?
- What's your vision?
- Will the negative state that you're in move you in that direction, or will it move you in another direction?

Then you should ask yourself these questions:

- Where is this situation headed, and is that okay?
- What do I intend to create?
- What's most important here?
- How might my negativity affect this relationship?
- Is my integrity at stake here?
- Could my health be more important than proving my point right now?

When you give up the need to be right, you expand your options and experience joy instead of distress. Only after finally seeing the big picture can you fully grasp that the negative situation you saw before was only a small part of the whole.

When you change your focus, you change your life!

5. You can drop the thought. You can simply refuse to indulge the negative thoughts. You can refuse to rehash them, replay them, or otherwise worship them. Warn yourself that when you neglect to drop the negative thought, you are choosing to *drink the poison*. Ironically, when you spew emotional venom toward another person, either verbally or silently, you are the one who receives the stiffest dose. As unfair as this seems to be, it is a sobering truth. Whatever you express to others is impressed within yourself. Instead of enabling negative thoughts to affect you, you can starve them by just letting them go.

You already have plenty of experience doing this. Let me explain. On many occasions, I'm sure you have experienced a distracting thought when you were in the middle of a business meeting or perhaps a romantic dinner with your spouse. Maybe you thought about an e-mail you needed to return or about the morning carpool plans. Quickly realizing that the thought was inappropriate, you just dropped it and continued with your evening. I know that many times I've been at the movies with my family and had thoughts of certain obligations or "to-dos" pop into my mind. I tell myself, *"This isn't the time. I can deal with that on Monday."* That little conversation almost instantly displaces the distracting thought. You've done exactly the same thing on many occasions because you wanted to or because you thought it was the right thing to do. In fact, you are constantly switching mental gears, but this switching happens largely as a reflex, not as deliberate intention.

I remember being in the middle of a little spat with my wife a number of years ago when we suddenly heard what sounded like our four-year-old falling out of his bed with a loud thud, closely followed by an unforgettable cry. Immediately, we halted the negativity and turned our attention to our child, thereby inadvertently activating the Law of Exchange. You and I can do that anytime we choose.

At times, we seem to think we have a right to negative thoughts. Instead of dismissing them, we embrace them. There's no benefit to doing that. You can drop the thoughts anytime you want; in fact, I'm giving you permission to do so! As one of my coaches shared with me, "That thought is not attached to you, Tommy; it's not glued to you. It is no more real than the dream you had last night." It's merely the power of habit that causes us to latch on to the negative and drop the positive.

Many people don't want to hear this because they have become accustomed to venting or periodically expressing their negativity to another person. Some people advocate venting because it lets off negative steam that has been mounting. But this cathartic benefit is often mitigated by the unintended consequence of the steam spreading to another person—usually someone they really care about. At best, the therapeutic benefit of venting is short lived. The negative emotion that was supposedly released rears its ugly head once again when prompted by a new event. At worst, an important relationship is damaged without addressing the source of the negativity.

What happens after venting that brings such relief? Once the person vents, he drops the thought and feels satisfied. Is venting a necessary prerequisite to dropping the thought? Could the drama of venting be bypassed? Maybe the venting is just a learned, popular ritual that helps us dump negative thoughts. What if you could break the link at the beginning? You could say, "It's not worth it." You could say, "I am responsible." You could give the other person the benefit of the doubt. As long as you are going to drop the thought eventually, why not drop it at the start, relax a little, and avoid damaging a relationship? It's worth thinking about. When you drop a negative thought, you preempt an emotional eruption. By "catching it early," you keep yourself in a resourceful state of mind, giving yourself the best shot at effectively solving problems, dealing with stress, and overcoming challenges.

6. You can retreat. Sometimes when you are in a down emotional state, the cause is a complete mystery. You may not be able to pinpoint anything that is specifically bothering you. In other cases, the trigger is quite obvious. Becoming adept at quickly recognizing these low moods is a skill worth developing. If you are unaware of your negative frame of mind, then the thoughts, words, and actions that follow can quickly fuel a negative spiral. It will consume significant time, energy, and goodwill to recover. In these situations, it is wise to consider the option of temporary retreat. Staying in the presence of others might inadvertently fuel your fire. Briefly withdrawing, especially from loved ones, allows the time-tested wisdom of "this

117

> In quietness and confidence shall be your strength.
> – Isaiah 30:15, NKJV

too shall pass" to kick in and start working to your advantage. Reminding yourself of this spiritual truth supplies a vision of closure and weakens the hold of negative emotions. It gives you something to hope for, a time to practice your faith.

From time to time, you may find it therapeutic to back

away, shut the door, be alone, and allow the fire of negative emotions to die down of its own accord. As children, most of us experienced this dynamic when we were sent to our rooms for a little while to cool off. However, you may have forgotten how well this works, unless you're still living with your parents. Though retreating may not resolve the situation, it limits the damage by *protecting you from yourself.* When you're feeling down or negative, the information transmitted from your brain is skewed to some degree. Trusting this faulty feedback leads only to poor decisions that make life worse. As the negative clouds pass, solutions seem much more apparent.

7. You can practice compassion. This is the master strategy for keeping you in the joy zone, especially when dealing with other people. Instead of suppressing or expressing negative emotions, you can extend compassion toward the person who seems to be the source of the negativity in the first place—even if it's you. How do you accomplish this?

Assume that other people are struggling or in pain. If they weren't, they wouldn't be acting so negatively, right? So, graciously give them the benefit of the doubt. Adopting this unusual perspective has helped my clients and me tremendously. Is this interpretation always true? Probably not, but what harm does it cause? Here are some much better questions to ask when you find yourself pulled toward negative thinking: Is this a useful belief? Is this a belief that will help me experience more joy? Will it cause me to be more empathetic? Will it help me get along better with others? Will it be constructive in my marriage or other relationships?

Earlier in this chapter, we talked about a car that cut me off on the freeway. What if I found out that the offending driver was rushing to the hospital to be with his daughter who was near death? Would that change my perspective? Absolutely. Could we assume that scenario, or something similar to it, is true every time we encounter a rude driver?

When people respond negatively, attribute it to something they are dealing with that you don't know about. They are likely just having a tough day. Maybe they are dealing with a heavy burden. Perhaps they just got dumped on by someone else, or maybe they got only two hours of sleep last night. It is helpful to remember that when someone treats you harshly, it says much more about him or her than about you. But how you respond reveals a lot about you.

When you practice compassion, you detach yourself from the situation and don't over-personalize it. The only downside is that at the end of your life, you may find out that your positive assumptions about other people weren't perfectly true. Even so, I propose that this is a belief worth having! Those years would still have been better lived than if you had assumed the worst about others. Do you agree? Because we learn our beliefs anyway, why not master this really beneficial one? Remember, when your interpretations change, so do your emotions.

Get curious. Being curious about the other person's story activates the Law of Exchange and also causes you to detach yourself from the situation and not take it so personally. For example, if I snapped at you, you might choose to think something like this: *I wonder what Tommy's story is? He doesn't seem exactly like himself today. I wonder what's going on there?* You become curious, almost like you're a researcher on a mission. The simple attempt at becoming interested in other people causes you to detach from negativity.

Remember that most negative outbursts are conditioned responses and not really so menacing. Write that on a card. Put it on your refrigerator, on the center console in your car, or on your screen saver. Use this understanding not to make excuses for yourself but to show compassion to others. Remind yourself that other people are living out scripts that were placed in their heads long before you ever met them. You may have acted as the trigger for their response, but you are not the source. Challenge yourself to become the type of individual who is not rattled by the reactions of others.

Realize that most stress and tension is just growth trying to take place. In fact, wherever there is an absence of productive friction, you are likely to find stagnation. And stagnation does not produce joy. This is an easy concept to grasp on a physical level. No one would ever expect to build stronger leg muscles without the resistance provided by weights and by running. Our muscles are pushed and stretched beyond previous limits, and once they recover from the stress, they become stronger than before. In a similar way, kids experience the pressure and tension of schoolwork, friendships, and family life. Without the strain and struggles of childhood, children would never mature into healthy, functioning adults.

On the mental and emotional plane, this concept is not so easily understood. We never graduate from emotional growth. To continue growing emotionally, we must experience resistance from time to time. Our response to it will determine whether we will grow closer to our full potential or further from it. Once you understand this growth principle, fear and insecurity begin to dissolve, and you are freed to reach the next level emotionally. Starting today, lighten up and affirm the truth about stress and tension. When you experience a difficult circumstance, consider it as an opportunity for growth. It will definitely help you live in the joy zone.

8. You can ask for God's help. As we've discussed, Romans 12:2 mentions how God can transform us by the renewing of our minds. He has the power to help us conquer our negative emotions, and he will help us when we ask. The psalms are great places to go when we feel angry or upset. Many of them model a healthy emotional progression from anger to peace, from despair to hope, from doubt to faith in God. Psalms 42 and 43 are great examples of this.

If you're reading this book, you're intentional about improving your potential for joy and probably have higher standards than the general population. But we all need to live with people who might not have such high standards. You can't control their emotions, but you can control yours. You'll never be perfect at dealing with your negative emotions, and that's fine because you can make tremendous progress—as long as you focus on what you *can* do instead of what you *can't*. If you are anything like me, your list of things that are possible is so long that you will never have time to get around to the things that are impossible!

Let me close this chapter with a key distinction and a corollary to the 4:8 Principle. I want you to say it over and over to yourself. I want you to post it where you will see it often. I want you to reflect on it and pray about it. This distinction changes the quality of your emotional life. It helps you develop the mental toughness, the mental resilience, and the mental power that leads you headfirst into a joy-filled life. Here it is: **Emotions don't reveal the quality of your life; they reveal the quality of your thinking at any particular moment.**

Joy unquestionably exposes 4:8 Thinking. Remember, this is your one shot at life. I want you to make it count! You *can* change your focus, and you *will* change your life!

A Prayer for Freedom

Heavenly Father,

I praise you for being everything that I need. Thank you for loving me perfectly. Whenever I struggle with the pain of dark emotions, fill me with the light of your presence. I trust you to put your healing hand where I need it most.

Please reveal any errors in my thinking that may be preventing me from experiencing life the way you intend. Protect me from the widespread mind games that can smother my potential for joy. Alert me to the truth of your

Word in all situations, particularly in the midst of negative distortions and exaggerations.

Remind me to focus on the big picture and what's really important, especially in my most cherished relationships. Fill my heart with compassion for the trouble, pain, and anguish that rule over the lives of so many people. Keep me relaxed and secure in your love so that I don't over-react to the conditioned negativity of others.

I know that your will for me does not include unproductive negative emotions. How great that is! Thank you for giving me power, love, and a sound mind so that I may live with joy all the days of my life.

In Jesus' name,

Amen

This One Thing I Do . . .

Beginning today, I increase my potential for joy by recognizing the big picture and responding compassionately, especially with those I love the most.

PART TWO SUMMARY

Developing Your Joy

- Forgive yourself and others without exception—and really mean it. This will be an ongoing process. Never let an old wound fester due to excessive attention.
- Contemplate often the wonderful future God has planned for you. Act with joy today, as if your full potential has already materialized.
- Release the need to hang on to thoughts that haven't worked well for you. Productive thinking disrupts unproductive thinking.
- Be aware that your emotions allow you to feel what you're thinking about. Far from being an objective indicator of the quality of your life, they reveal the quality of your thinking. To make wise decisions, let your goals—not your emotions—guide you.

Power, Love, and a Sound Mind

The 4:8 Challenge

1. In what ways could you take better care of your mind and body so that they accurately represent how valuable you truly are?
2. What does your self-talk today reveal about your expectations for tomorrow? Whom in your life can you trust for honest feedback in this area?
3. Which "really awful thoughts" can you relate to the

most? Which RAIs do you intend to exterminate first? Why?

4. In what ways have you recently highlighted the wrong things (such as weaknesses, mistakes, faults) in an important relationship? How did this approach work for you? What is the secret to bringing out the best in others?

PART THREE

GUARD YOUR HEART

Defending Your Joy

CHAPTER 7

YOUR PERSONAL FIREWALL

Developing Habits to Protect Your Heart

Guard your heart above all else, for it determines the course of your life.
– Proverbs 4:23, NLT

In part one, we laid the groundwork for the 4:8 Principle and talked about the power of controlling your thoughts. In part two, we discussed how you can improve your self-concept and take command of your emotional life. Now, in part three, you will learn why it is critical to defend your mind from negative exposures that interfere with the 4:8 Principle and diminish your opportunities for a joy-filled life. Exposure refers to anything you come in contact with during your lifetime. From inside the womb right up to the present moment, your character has been and will continue to be molded by your surroundings. If you neglect to take strategic control of these exposures, you'll find it's like building on the sand. Things may seem fine for a while, but ultimately your full potential can begin to crumble under the stress and storms of life.

As a child of God, you are called to be a faithful steward of your thought life. God calls you to keep yourself pure, not to fill your mind with things that go against his law and desires, "so that you may become blameless and pure, children of God without fault in a crooked and depraved generation, in which you shine like stars in the universe" (Philippians 2:15, NIV). *Guard your heart* means to be intentional about your exposures, so that as you strengthen your mind, you simultaneously increase your capacity to serve others and affect the world in positive ways. Realize that everything you read, watch, or listen to and especially the people you choose to associate with either bring you closer to joy or nudge you further away. Remember, you can point the spotlight of your attention wherever you like.

Protecting the "Software" of Your Mind

Several years ago when I was relocating The 1% Club to a new office building closer to my home, I made the decision to upgrade our company server at the same time. Unfortunately, the installation did not go as planned, and the firewall was not set up properly, rendering it ineffective and useless. During the very first weekend of operation, when we were mistakenly exposed to the rest of the Internet universe, we were invaded by some mysterious computer programs that borrowed our server and used it as a launching pad for more than 250,000 spam messages. Upon arriving at the office on Monday morning, we found a largely dysfunctional server overwhelmed with error messages and incapable of handling even the simplest of our business needs. We could not e-mail, use our contact database, or access key research files. It was a mess.

Unaware of exactly what had happened, our informa-

tion systems consultants worked to repair the obvious prob
lems, not knowing that we had also contracted, and spread
to some of our customers, several viruses throughout the
weekend. To make matters worse, we had been fingered as
the source of a massive quantity of unsolicited e-mails that
we had nothing to do with. This caused The 1% Club to
be "blacklisted" or automatically disconnected from some
of the world's largest Internet service providers, who were
trying to block spammers from infiltrating their systems. As
a result of allowing this trash into our hard drive, we were
unable to communicate by e-mail with some of our best cli
ents for up to a year, and we inadvertently caused a host of
other technical glitches as well. That was a trying experience,
but it presents a valuable lesson about how we can be cor-
rupted by something less than desirable. **We often allow
negative ideas and others' opinions to corrupt our
potential for joy,** sometimes even infecting the people
we love most in the process. It doesn't have to be this way!
If you are ready and willing, you can construct your own
"firewall" and protect the software of your mind.

131

Engineered for Joy

To experience maximum joy, you must first improve the
quality of your thinking. That was the emphasis of earlier
chapters. You are where you are at this point in your life
because of the dominating thoughts you have allowed to
occupy your mind. Your health, your marriage, your career,
and all the other aspects of your life are colored by the
quality of your mental diet. These habitual thought patterns, accumulated over a lifetime, trigger your actions and

determine your quality of life, even though you are not consciously aware of most of them. As we've discussed, we can train ourselves to be more deliberate about our thoughts. But another way to minimize negative thought patterns is to purposely remove ourselves from negative situations. In this section, you will be encouraged and equipped to become intentional and purposeful with your exposures.

What you let in your heart shapes what you believe, expect, and do.

132

Sometimes your thoughts are triggered by your surroundings. Sometimes they are triggered by your memory, and other times they are brought about through your imagination. In some cases, a particular thought just seems to come out of nowhere. So if you are to keep your mind on godly things—if you are to dwell on what is lovely, pure, gracious, and just—then it is critical that you have a plan. Choosing to wing it is the same as choosing to fall short of your full potential. Why in the world would you want to do that?

In Philippians, Paul lays out a clear game plan for what we should think about. It is a challenge, but if you and I could not accomplish it, he would not have suggested it. If you believe that your thinking is important and you accept Paul's advice, what is the next step? How do you get to the place where living the 4:8 Principle becomes second nature? You are engineered for joy and delight, but it's easy to unknowingly program yourself for stagnation and mediocrity. Because most of your thinking comes from your exposures, it is easy to become overly influenced by your surroundings. That's why it's so important to protect yourself. Let's look at some specific reasons.

You Should Guard Your Heart Because . . .

1. THOUGHTS ARE CAUSES, AND CIRCUMSTANCES ARE THE EFFECTS.

Surprisingly, many people have this backward; they believe that circumstances cause their thoughts. However, if you are dissatisfied with the conditions of your life, you now know what you need to do: Hold up your circumstances as a mirror and figure out what types of thoughts could be causing the blemishes you spot in the reflection. After all, you would never blame the mirror for what it reflects back to you. Your life today corresponds with your thoughts from the past. Virtually all causation is mental. If you want to produce a specific outcome in your life, you must trace back from that outcome and identify the types of thoughts that would produce such a result. For every effect in your life, there is a thought or crop of thoughts that are responsible.

What you sow in thought, either useful or useless, manifests itself sooner or later in your circumstances. As your coach, I want to encourage you to start living more consistently with a central law of the Bible: Whatever you sow, you shall also reap (see Galatians 6:7). Put another way, "whoever sows sparingly will also reap sparingly, and whoever sows generously will also reap generously" (2 Corinthians 9:6, NIV).

This law works 24/7 everywhere in the world, for sinner and saint alike. Specifically, if you want to reap more joy, you must plant joyful thoughts—and lots of them. It is simply impossible to produce a result that has not first been formed in thought. There's no need to take my word for it. When you look through the all-time best seller, you will have God's word on it. God promises that all your actions produce reactions, that what you sow in thought or deed, you shall certainly reap. Consider Matthew 7:2, "For in the same way you judge others, you will be judged, and with the measure you use, it will be measured to you" (NIV); or Job 4:8, "Those who plow iniquity and sow trouble reap the same" (ESV). In Matthew 12:34, Jesus asks, "How can you who are evil say anything good? For out of the overflow of the heart the mouth speaks" (NIV).

Just because a cause is not readily apparent does not mean there is no cause. Often there is such a time lag between the plane of thought and the visible plane that the connection to causation is blurred. However, you can determine causation by careful study of your thought life. Because your thoughts directly or indirectly produce your circumstances, monitor them closely.

2. YOUR SUBCONSCIOUS MIND REMEMBERS EVERYTHING!

"Guard your heart above all else, for it determines the course of your life" (Proverbs 4:23, NLT). The phrase "the heart," as used in the Bible, most closely represents what present-day psychology refers to as the subconscious mind. King Solomon, who wrote most of the book of Proverbs, was very much ahead of the curve when it came to wisdom, and this particular subject matter was no exception. Whatever gets into your subconscious stays there. This falls into the "scary but true" category! Any emotionally charged image or idea that is repeatedly held in your conscious mind is processed as a command by your subconscious mind. The *dominant impressions* in your subconscious mind sooner or later become the *dominant expressions* in your conditions. Because the subconscious mind does not distinguish between truth and fantasy, it accepts input without regard to present reality. In effect, the subconscious is a perfect servant, complying with the instructions that you give it. Once again, this can be either good or bad news for you, depending on whether those instructions are positive or negative. The more you claim your troubles as permanent fixtures, the less you enjoy life today. Yet the more you affirm God's great plans and blessings for the future, the more fully alive you'll be in the current moment.

135

On the defensive side, "guarding your heart" means protecting your subconscious from limiting, joy-suppressing beliefs. On the offensive side, it means deliberately supplying your subconscious mind with godly, potential-releasing orders. When you follow Philippians 4:8, you displace self-defeating thinking patterns and furnish your subconscious with clear, unambiguous directions for the future. If you are doing your best to follow the 4:8 Principle, then you will eventually reap better fruit than someone who does not do so. Your responsibility is to convince your subconscious that the joyful conditions you desire *already* exist. I know that sounds a bit odd, but stick with me a moment longer. Is there a secret that could make this possible? Well, it may not be a secret, but there is definitely an answer, and it is *faith.* **Authentic joy can always be recognized by the**

indispensable leap in faith that precedes it. You can activate this faith by expectantly aligning your attitude with your prayers in advance of any tangible reason to do so.

3. YOUR MIND IS A SPONGE.

Think of your mind as a sponge. It acts on what it soaks up. And when it is squeezed, guess what comes out? You're right! Only one thing can possibly come out, and that is what you put in. Being aware of this dynamic can mitigate the damage negative exposures inflict on your personal growth. Most people simply don't pay any attention to their exposures. Instead, they just soak them up. They listen to whatever happens to be playing on the radio. They watch the TV programs that the networks promote. They read the books everyone else is reading. They skim through the magazines left in reception areas. They get engaged in whatever headlines pop in front of their eyes. They contribute to "ain't it awful?" conversations and add to idle gossip.

They take a casual and reactive approach to what they are feeding their minds, just as many take the same low-end approach in feeding their bodies. When you put garbage in your body, you pay the unpleasant short- and long-term consequences. When you allow garbage in your mind, you clog your potential for joy, satisfaction, and lasting success as well. **If junk goes in, then sooner or later junk must come out.** It's impossible to avoid this. If you are passively ingesting what our culture routinely shovels in, then you will gradually become conformed to this world. You will *not* be renewed by the transforming of your mind (see Romans 12:2) unless you make a deliberate and contrarian effort to do so. When you put good in, then good comes out. This is God's law of causality.

You are the gatekeeper of your mind. To experience a life full of joy, you must reject the negatives and protect the positives God has placed or has promised to place in your life. **Those who experience more joy don't necessarily have more to be joyful about; they just think differently.** This option is available to you as well. Here are three strategies you can use immediately to help you erect a fortress around your mind. Remember, every moment matters. Think of the habits described below as the guardrails of a joy-filled heart.

137

Habit One: Feed Yourself with Positive Mental Nutrition

To insulate your heart from negative messages that would deplete your potential for joy, you must feed your mind what I call *positive mental nutrition*. This refers to deliberate, 4:8-certified inputs that come from what you read, watch, and listen to on a consistent basis. To live an uncommon, joy-filled life, deliberately immerse yourself in wise, inspiring, and uplifting thoughts on a preplanned schedule. Ask yourself, "How are my reading, listening, Web-surfing, and TV habits different from those of non-Christians?" Start with the Bible and expand from there. Read books that challenge your ruts and prod you to escape from the ordinary. Read books that raise interesting questions and inspire you to live and give in exceptional ways. Read books that help you grow in wisdom as a parent. Listen to CDs that remind you of your true potential and the possibilities before you. Listen to the life stories of the people you admire the most and aspire to be like. Listen to audio downloads that equip you to be a stronger husband or wife. Load your iPod with your favorite sermons and with music that moves you. Reading books and listening to CDs about faith, life, and love does more than expand your knowledge base. It also keeps your growth at the forefront of your mind, and *growth contributes to joy.* The very act of seeking new insights drives out stale thinking. When you're reading and listening to great ideas, then by default, you can't be filling your mind with mediocre inputs.

138

Watch television only in moderation. Be highly intentional. Pick your programs in advance and view them on your timetable. Consider using a digital video recorder such as TiVo so you can view programs without commercials. There are plenty of excellent programs to watch if you do a little detective work and scan your cable or satellite provider's weekly schedule. I encourage my 1% Club clients to watch only sports and news live; everything else can be recorded for future playback at a more convenient time. And of course, the news is often toxic and should be consumed in the most condensed format available. Besides, contemporary television news contains much more commentary and far fewer facts than ever before.

The Power of Accumulation

Long before digital video recorders existed, I would have certain clients record their favorite television programs on videotape for one week. There were no restrictions on what they could watch; the only rule was that they had to record it before they watched it. Instead of watching live TV, they would engage in other activities with the idea that they would "catch up" with their favorite shows over the weekend. You can probably guess what happened. In most cases, they would never find the time to watch last week's programs. This little exercise eased the entertainment dependency a bit. You might give this approach a try and see how it works for your family.

Let's look at television, using a little bit of math. If you or your kids watch two hours each day, that will translate into thirty full days of TV watching over the next year, and forty-three weeks over the next ten years. If you substitute just fifteen minutes of that TV time per day and apply it to reading, devotions, exercise, prayer, sleep, a romantic stroll under the stars, or any other life-enhancing activity, that adds up to four full days over the next year and almost six weeks over the next ten years. According to A. C. Nielsen Co., the average American watches more than four hours of TV each day, which translates into two months of non-stop TV watching per year, and nine complete years of TV over a sixty-five-year life span.

Think of this as the principle of accumulation. Small things add up to big things over time. It doesn't happen over night, but we are all accumulating something. What about you? What are you accumulating?

You attract into your life the people, ideas, and circumstances that correspond with your habitual thinking. And three years from now, your family life, health, relationships, and finances will reflect what you have been feeding yourself. You become what you think about most.

Habit Two: Start the Day with Joy

Focus on joy the first fifteen minutes after you wake up. Think of what I call the First Fifteen as your "early morning joy ritual" (EMJR). What you do first thing in the morning sets the emotional tone for the entire rest of the day. Do you wake up full of anticipation like a little child on Christmas Day? If your

> Realize that everything you watch, read, or listen to either brings you closer to God or nudges you further away.

140

morning doesn't start with joy, you will find it difficult to make a comeback later in the day. First thing in the morning, before your mind gets cluttered with the busyness and obligations of the day, is the perfect time to work on your "joy software."

How do you currently start the day? Motivational legend Zig Ziglar once joked with his audience that he wakes up in the morning and reads from his Bible and then the local paper so that he knows what both sides are up to. How about you? What do you feed your mind in the first fifteen minutes after awaking? Do the first fifteen minutes of your morning glorify God and set the foundation for a joy-filled day? To start your day with joy, first make a decision to do so. Then make a simple plan. Develop a list of one to three quick things you could do in fifteen minutes that are consistent with a joy-filled life. If you have to, wake up fifteen minutes early to seize this opportunity.

To expand on the Law of Accumulation, mentioned above, if you invest just fifteen minutes each morning in preparation for joy, it will add up to seven and a half hours in the first thirty days alone. The compounding effect in a year is even more shocking. But if the best part of waking up is Folgers in your cup, then we need to talk directly!

Here are eight questions to consider as you work to build your morning momentum:

1. What could I read, watch, or listen to during the first fifteen minutes I'm awake?
2. What should I avoid reading, watching, or listening to?
3. How could I prepare myself for this EMJR the night before?
4. What could I tell myself the instant I wake up every morning?
5. What should I avoid telling myself the instant I wake up?
6. How could I intensify my gratitude in the First Fifteen?
7. How could I use prayer and Scripture?
8. How could I use the 4:8 Questions?

Of course, you are free to extend your EMJR beyond the First Fifteen. Many of my clients have expanded morning routines that last ninety minutes or longer. With the extra time, you could incorporate physical exercise, positive affirmation, vision review, and other elements of a joy-filled life.

Do you believe God wants you to launch into each day with joy? I believe your potential for joy begins with daily quiet time. If you're going to "seek first the kingdom of

God," as we're taught in Matthew 6:33 (NKJV), then it makes good sense to schedule this appointment with your Creator first thing in the morning. After all, could there be a more important appointment all day long? If you're ever tempted to say that you don't have time for this solitude with God, ask yourself bluntly, "What could I possibly do with that time that would bring me any greater benefit?" Minutes invested in praying for wisdom will save days spent in overcoming mistakes. To advance in joy, first retreat with God.

Put first things first, and your whole day will be securely built on the rock of God's promises. Remember, **your potential for joy is limited only by your preparation for joy.**

Habit Three: Seal the Day with Joy

Now that you've taken care of the First Fifteen, I want to encourage you to approach the Final Fifteen in much the same way. Your subconscious mind has its guard down and is very receptive to suggestive influences in the last few minutes before you fall asleep, so this is the second daily opportunity you want to take advantage of. The inputs you allow into your relaxed mind right before bedtime are more readily impressed into your subconscious than those scattered throughout the rest of the day. Remember, what gets *impressed* in your heart gets *expressed* in your circumstances.

How do you end each day right now? Do you end with the late-night news? If so, what is getting impressed in your mind as a result? Do you end the day chastising yourself for what you didn't get accomplished? Do you end the day worrying about tomorrow's to-do list or the state of your finances? Have you ever ended an evening on a really bad note with your spouse or child? If so, what do you think got impressed in both of your minds? **The absolute worst time to be negative, to be discouraged, to argue, or to deal with junk is right before bedtime!**

I encourage you to carve out the Final Fifteen and make it a special and purposeful time. Like an oasis from daily stress, the Final Fifteen should become the most refreshing and restorative part of the day. How could you use the Final Fifteen to exploit your potential for joy? Could you ask the 4:8 Questions? Could you imagine your vision and goals as already accomplished? Could you study the Bible or read an inspirational book? Could you pray with or share a special kiss with your spouse? Could you review your victories from the day? If you did any or all of the above, what kinds of messages would get impressed on your mind? Brainstorm some other ideas. What is the most fabulously positive thing you could do each night before you drift to sleep?

> Do not let the sun go down on your wrath.
> – Ephesians 4:26, NKJV

One of the best things I've learned to do in the Final Fifteen is surrender my subconscious to God. There is no one way to do this. I just ask him to cleanse me of any self-defeating thoughts that I may have allowed to "set up camp" and replace them with thoughts that would be pleasing to him. When I am faced with a problem or working on a big goal, such as writing this book, I specifically ask God to work through my subconscious as I sleep. I try to release my preconceived notions and pray for his ideas to become my creativity, for his words to become my words. I encourage you to give this a try in your own style. When you do, I believe it will become a fixture in your Final Fifteen.

A Prayer for Discernment

Father God,

Help me to live intentionally, particularly when it comes to what I read, watch, and listen to on a consistent basis. Guide me to allow into my soul only those words, sounds, and images that support who you want me to become. Reveal to me the role I must play in guarding the door of my heart. Keep me from becoming careless about the inputs of each day and the effect my environment has on my potential. Because I soak up my surroundings, show me if I have any current exposures that are not pleasing to you, and lead me to make changes so I can experience your presence in a deeper and fuller way.

Inspire me, hour by hour, to fill my mind with everything good. Remind me that everything counts, and that what I sow, I sooner or later will certainly reap.

In Jesus' name,

Amen

144

This One Thing I Do . . .

Beginning today, I increase my potential for joy by thoughtfully planning and using the First Fifteen and Final Fifteen of each day.

CHAPTER 8

JUNK-PROOF YOUR MIND

Strategies for a Healthy Mind

Every experience in life, everything with which we have come in contact in life is a chisel which has been cutting away at our life statue, molding, modifying, and shaping it. We are part of all we have met. Everything we have seen, heard, felt, or thought has had its hand in molding and shaping us.

– Orison Swett Marden

We all recognize the need for a healthy body, and we certainly accept the benefits of physical exercise. Exercise will keep your energy level high, strengthen your immunity, improve your mood, and reduce the effects of negative stress, to name just a few benefits. As we discussed in chapter 4, a healthy, functional body is a key factor in shaping your self-concept.

Most of us also recognize the need for a healthy mind. But that seems a little more difficult to define than a healthy body. What exactly is a *healthy* mind? Could it be the result of thinking consistently with Philippians 4:8? Consider your mind healthy if it works *for* you instead of against you. A healthy mind serves up thoughts that release your full potential. A healthy mind keeps your *attention* on your *intention.* It looks ahead and harbors a clear vision for the future. **A healthy mind produces joy, like a healthy body produces energy.** It agrees with God's promises. And a healthy, disciplined mind craves direction, growth, and challenge.

To achieve a healthy body, you know you must eat the proper quantity and variety of nutrient-dense foods. You must drink lots of pure water. You must exercise your heart, lungs, and muscles. You should consider taking high-quality supplements, and you should get ample sleep as well. But what can you do to achieve a healthy mind? What can you do to keep your thoughts fixed on what is lovely, pure, gracious, and just? How do you stay mentally fit?

Think about it like this: If your goal is to lose weight, then you know what you have to do. You must change your diet. You have to decide in advance what kind of food and drink is consistent with your weight-loss goals and what kind is not. And for this change in diet to be effective in the long run, you'll probably need to remove the junk food and unhealthy snacks from your environment and replace them with healthy, energy-producing choices. Otherwise, trying to lose weight will remain "trying" indefinitely. One of the most critical but least emphasized elements of a successful weight-loss program is aligning your refrigerator and cupboards with your health goals. If you intend to lose weight but continue to stock the same unhealthy foods in your home, then the diet will no doubt be short lived.

Likewise, if your goal is to experience more joy, you have to change your mental diet. If you are serious about making progress in this area, you must alter the exposures that trigger negativity in the first place. You must synchronize your mental refrigerator with your goal of maximum joy. You must toss the junk thoughts that oppose God's promises, and instead, stock your surroundings with joy-producing inputs that encourage right thinking and discourage negative, lazy thinking. Be aware that this is an ongoing process. If you throw these items out but restock with negative influences a few hours later, then your progress will be neutralized.

Over the years, I have had a number of clients who chronically struggled with weight loss because they could not get their environment under control. In some cases, they were committed but their spouse was not, and so tantalizing junk food was constantly all around them. Each evening as they returned home, they were led into "nutrition temptation." That is no excuse, of course. You can reach your fitness goals even in the presence of the wrong food; it just requires an extra dose of discipline. I have observed, though, that over the long haul, a supportive environment beats an exertion of discipline hands down.

Are you ready to junk-proof your mental environment? It will require some throwing out and some bringing in. Fortunately, this is not an all-or-nothing proposition. With weight loss, some of my clients want to get really lean with single-digit body fat percentages, and others have a less extreme ideal. It is the same with your mental diet. Ask yourself, *How mentally lean do I want to be?* How much joy do you think you can stand? How much junk are you willing to put up with? What do you really want? What does God want for you? In chapter 7, we looked at *why* you must protect your mind, as well as three habits to start you on your way to more positive inputs. In the rest of this chapter, you will learn seven practical strategies for protecting your mind.

Strategy One: Focus on the Right Relationships

Whenever I speak to an audience of teenagers, I share a powerful visual about the importance of choosing friends wisely. I get a volunteer to allow me to try to pull him up on the stage using just one arm. I try to pick someone whom I am unable to lift with just one arm. After a few exaggerated efforts, I ask the teenager to try to pull me down off the stage using just a pinky finger. Even though in most cases I have a nice weight advantage, I am easily pulled off the stage with the power of one little finger. The young adults are a bit surprised and get the message quickly: **In life, it's far easier to be pulled down than lifted up.**

Now that I have their attention, I tell them that every relationship they have, for the rest of their lives, will be doing one of those two things—lifting them up or pulling them down. Judging from the letters I receive, this brief demonstration makes a lasting impact. Even though that visual is intended for teenagers, it seems to resonate with adults just as deeply. It is so easy to let our friends pick us rather than to assertively choose our friends. It is easier, especially for children, to gravitate toward those who accept us rather than those who will draw the best out of us.

How about you? Are you being sharpened by the right people? Do the people you spend most of your time with amplify the joy in your life? As Paul writes in 1 Corinthians 15:33, "Don't be fooled . . . , 'bad company corrupts good character'" (NLT). In Proverbs 27:17, we are reminded that one person sharpens another just as iron sharpens iron. The individuals you habitually choose to associate with will influence who you become as a person more than any other single factor. You will inevitably take on the habits, attitudes, beliefs, and even the mannerisms of the people you surround yourself with. You will be either sharpened or dulled by your choice of associations. Keep your goals far away from people who shrink dreams and who encourage the enemy called "good enough." Instead, get around people who challenge you to constantly stretch, raise your standards, and pursue your biggest dreams.

If you hang around people who have no real vision or who limit God with their own caustic attitudes, you will eventually become just like them. Negative people poison your outlook, exhaust your energy, and chip away at your potential for joy. If you associate on a regular basis with people who whine, gossip, condemn, and commiserate, then the inescapable fact is that sooner or later you will resemble them. It's highly unlikely that you will even notice this evolution because changes in character happen so gradually. Character change, either good or bad, sneaks up on you like weight gain—one tiny ounce at a time. People do not punch, kick, and drag you off course; if that were the case, you would fight back and protect yourself. Rather, they nudge you just a little bit, then a little bit more, then a hair more, until you are finally "pulled off the stage." **When people with different values hang out together, somebody ultimately changes.**

If you want to live the 4:8 Principle and maximize your

joy, you must make the shift to investing time with the right people—individuals who lift you up and produce a godly return in your life. How exactly do you determine which people are the right ones to invite into your inner circle? Well, it all depends on your particular vision, but if your aim is a joy-filled life, here are seven thought triggers to get you started.

Invest more time with people who look like this:

152

1. Their character and integrity are equal to or greater than your own.
2. They share your faith, or even better, they are further along in their relationship with God.
3. Their lives demonstrate the joy-filled fruit of their faith.
4. You'd like your children to grow up and be similar to them.
5. They hold you accountable and ask you the tough questions that are avoided by the majority.
6. They draw the best out of you and remind you that God is doing exciting things through you.
7. They are sincerely committed to being positively sharpened by their exposure to you!

Lifting and Pulling

From time to time, you will encounter situations where you will have no choice but to be right smack in the middle of negative people and stressful, turbulent relationships. During the breaks at most of my public seminars, I speak with at least a couple of attendees who are looking for advice on dealing with the fallout spawned by these unavoidable negative exposures. Apparently, the topic of positive relationships strikes a chord with a lot of people. Usually the question goes something like this: "How can you minimize the damage if there is no way to eliminate the exposure?" or "What do you do if you have to be around negative people on a regular basis, such as certain family members or coworkers?"

Essentially, the answer to either question is the same. Remember that life is far too short to be held captive by the negativity of others. Whatever you can do to proactively organize your lifestyle around positive, upbeat, and growth-oriented individuals will serve you well. That being said, there are a couple of steps you can take to minimize the damage from these joy bandits.

153

First and foremost, **become alert to who is lifting you up and who is pulling you down.** This simple recognition raises your guard and reduces the spread of negative attitudes. To heighten your awareness, divide all your relationships into

Are your associations in sync with your ambitions?

three categories. Label the first category "Red Relationships," and list the most negative, small-thinking people in your life. Whenever feasible, avoid these red relationships. The next category is "Yellow Relationships," which includes people you should hang out with in moderation. The third category is "Green Relationships," which are the most positive, joyful people in your life *right now* plus the people you *hope* will become a bigger part of your life in the near future. To engage the 4:8 Principle, focus on deliberately increasing the quantity of time you invest with these individuals.

Next, give the "Oreo Cookie Technique" a try. No, this doesn't mean you give the offending person an Oreo and ask him or her to go away. It means that when you must be around a negative person, you inoculate yourself before the contact with ultra-positive exposures and you disinfect yourself afterward in much the same way. The purpose of the first "cookie" is to strengthen your immunity. You could pray, read something unusually inspiring, exercise vigorously, meditate, or speak with a joy-filled friend, to name just a few options. Then you head into the stressful situation—the cream filling—with a full tank of joy. Following the encounter, you cleanse yourself with some extraordinarily positive inputs—the second cookie. Try this and see for yourself how a little forethought can preserve or even multiply your joy. Make this simple discipline a routine operating principle in your life. You can counteract any destructive exposure with an immediate injection of positive mental nutrition.

Keep in mind that dealing with negative, sour people is not pleasant work, but it is work that must be done. Severing the influence of such individuals can certainly be inconvenient and even distasteful at times. However, neglecting to protect your heart produces consequences that are far more unpleasant in the long run.

Strategy Two: Memorize Scripture

Memorizing Scripture is one of the simplest and surest methods for cleansing, renewing, strengthening, and guarding your mind. In chapter 5, we mentioned an important psychological principle: **Your conscious mind can hold only one thought at a time, positive _or_ negative. The only way to eliminate a negative or counter-productive thought is to replace it with a positive, empowering thought.** This is where memorization comes in. By committing Scripture verses to memory, you begin the process of crowding out negative, limiting thoughts and replacing them with the tremendous power and potential of God's promises. Your greatest asset is God working in you and through you, and this is best accomplished by allowing God's Word to abide in you. When you allow God's Word to permanently occupy your heart and mind, it inevitably shapes your desires and goals. And, as Jesus says in John 15:7, "If you remain in me and my words remain in you, you may ask for anything you want, and it will be granted!" (NLT). When you explore the Bible and memorize passages that address important issues in your life, you will be astonished by the joy and strength you receive as a result.

Start by writing down one verse each week on a three-by-five card and carrying it with you for the entire week, rereading it ten to twenty times a day. After a year, you'll have fifty-two nuggets of wisdom and inspiration stored away in your own spiritual medicine cabinet. (See the Afterword for a sampling of a dozen verses to get you started.)

Strategy Three: Personalize Bible Passages

Put yourself into the pages of the Bible by inserting your name and the pronouns _I, me,_ and _mine_ into your favorite inspirational verses. This technique will help you take possession of the abundance of spiritual gems that God has laid out for you in the pages of the Bible. Here are some examples of how I personalize Scripture:

- Christ has come so that I, Tommy Newberry, might have life and have it more abundantly. (John 10:10)
- The Kingdom of God is within me. (Luke 17:21)
- God has not given me a spirit of fear, but of power, and of love, and of a sound mind. (2 Timothy 1:7)
- In Christ I live, move, and have my being. (Acts 17:28)
- God is my refuge and strength, a very present help in trouble. (Psalm 46:1)
- I, Tommy Newberry, am transformed by the renewing of my mind. (Romans 12:2)

Try it for yourself! The possibilities are virtually endless.

Strategy Four: Affirm God's Goodness

To affirm God's goodness means to declare with conviction the goodness, abundance, and joy that God has promised his children. Conversely, *do not affirm* what you *do not want* in your life. Refuse to get cornered into conversations involving cynicism, doubt, fear, worry, or gossip. Typically, **self-talk refers to your habitual inner voice, which becomes evident to others when you speak.** As a rule, it is quite contagious. Just as you might cringe on an airplane when you hear coughing, sneezing, and other signs of sickness nearby, you should stay alert to the negativity of those around you. Do not let others contaminate your mind with their pessimism and idle words. Practically speaking, this means talking to yourself and others only about the conditions you desire and the things God wants for you.

In Matthew 12:37, Jesus teaches, "By your words you will be justified, and by your words you will be condemned" (NKJV). We are responsible for what we say. Practicing affirmations retrains your automatic self-talk so that it is in harmony with a joy-filled life. Think of an affirmation as the perfect expression of faith. **To affirm simply means to build up or reinforce that which you want in your life.** It is about aligning your speech with your trust in God. An affirmation is a joy tool that helps you build your character, your personality, your attitude—in fact, your very existence here on earth. What are you building with the inner dialogue that races through your secret place? The words you use are like seeds that, once planted, begin to shape the world you see.

When my second son, Mason, was about three years old, we would often spend a lot of time together building things. He especially liked building Lego towers because the potential for new and different designs was limited only by his imagination (and the number of pieces in the set). One afternoon, we began the construction process with Mason in charge and closely supervising every placement I made with the pieces. Pretty impressed with the progress of the building, I glanced at Mason and noticed a rather mischievous look in his eye—which was quickly followed by a sweeping karate chop straight through the center of our efforts of the last fifteen minutes. Of course, this demolished our tower, but it produced great laughter in both of us. Seconds after destroying our first structure, Mason was quickly picking up the pieces and beginning to assemble building number two. This process of building and tearing down continued.

Our spiritual growth and development often mirrors this toddler-style fun. We often make great strides toward our goals, only to wreck that progress with self-inflicted sabotage, forcing us to start over once again. The wrecking ball may take different forms—negative self-talk, fear, neglect, procrastination, worry, and so forth—but it demonstrates how important it is to get out of our own way.

Whether you realize it or not, you are always affirming something because you are always thinking. More accurately, you are constantly either building or demolishing. The key question is, What are you affirming? Would you be affirming the same thing if God were physically standing next to you, encouraging you?

Unlike Ivory soap, most of us are not 99.44 percent pure with our thoughts. Instead, we dilute our potential by thinking first one thing, then another—thinking of God's grace, then feeling guilty about our faults; thinking of God's awesome power, then talking about how we cannot seem to get rid of this little bug. We think about abundance and then seconds later worry over the bills. We are often like a driver frantically shifting from drive to reverse, to drive and back to reverse, with no hope of moving very far ahead. This barrage of mental contradictions locks us into whatever behavior has already become entrenched as a habit. Try as we may on the outside, we soon return to the behavior triggered from the inside. It does not have to be this way.

Here are three keys to verbalizing God's promises:

Key One: Pay Attention

Become highly sensitive to what you think about most often. What you say to yourself and others provides the biggest clue as to the quality of your thought life.

Key Two: Reinforce

Remind yourself that nothing is too good to be true for a child of the King. God wants you to prosper and have every good thing. Do not block his generosity with unprofitable talk.

Key Three: Filter and Replace

Swap all self-defeating words, phrases, and expressions with their positive opposite. Practice using the 4:8 Principle in almost any situation:

- On the phone
- With your mate
- With your coworkers
- With your kids
- With friends
- At social events

Talk only about what is "good, pure, lovely, and worthy of praise." Refuse to say anything that is unbecoming of a child of God. Make everything that comes out of your mouth first pass through the filter of Philippians 4:8. If you cannot say something positive, silence is the best alternative.

Strategy Five: Visualize God's Blessings!

God designed you and me with the mental capability to envision a better future, to see and imagine things as they *could be* rather than just as they are. This is most apparent when we pray. We are always led to pray for something better, not for something worse. In effect, as human beings, God has given us the power to create what we visualize, but most people visualize only what already exists. This concept is so simple yet profound that it is worth repeating: **We have been given the power to have what we visualize, but we tend to visualize only that which we already have.** And as long as you fix your mind only on what you currently have, you will very likely receive nothing more. If you persistently hold mental pictures of the past and present, you won't travel far from those images in reality.

> Nurture great thoughts, for you will never go higher than your thoughts.
> – Benjamin Disraeli

160

Unquestionably, a clear vision for the future is a key prerequisite for reaching your full potential here on earth. Without such vision, individuals, couples, families, organizations, and entire civilizations drift and meander, squandering opportunities for growth and positive influence that can spring only from a specific destination and path for the future. If you do not bother to activate this God-given inner power to shape your future, then it's very easy to lose the joy and enthusiasm that God intended for all his children. This power to visualize can be used or discarded; it is your choice.

Don't let the word *visualization* intimidate you. It simply refers to *seeing future possibilities*. At one time or another, we have all practiced visualization, either randomly or purposefully. Young baseball players visualize playing in the big leagues someday. Many young women clearly visualize the details of their wedding day long before it happens. Newly married couples frequently envision their future children playing throughout the house. Business leaders visualize and rehearse important presentations well ahead of delivering them to clients. Successful entrepreneurs visualize new customers and the rewards that correspond with expanding their service and contribution in the marketplace. We all have the capability to envision a wonderful future or an improved condition in our lives. Unfortunately, many people spend far more time visualizing what they don't want than what they do want. Then they make decisions based on the fear and worry these mental images generate.

I encourage you not to approach the visualization process randomly or haphazardly. If you are willing to train your mind, you will be much better prepared to carry out the work God has called you to do. Your responsibility is to deliberately feed your mind crisp, vivid pictures of the person God wants you to become. This starts with practicing the 4:8 Principle. Certainly, God's vision for your future is lovely, excellent, and worthy of praise—even well beyond your imagination!

To get started, set aside four or five minutes every day to visualize yourself, in as much detail as possible, living a joy-filled life. See yourself fully alive, loving your work and having a strong, positive impact. Envision yourself completely engaged and energized at home with your family.

Rehearse these ideal scenarios frequently with as much clarity as possible. Visualization is used by successful people in all fields, especially in athletics, entertainment, and more recently in leading-edge hospitals throughout the world. I devote an entire chapter to the discipline of visualization in my book *Success Is Not an Accident*.

Visualization works because it relies on the human brain's tendency to fulfill its most dominant thought. This is part of God's perfect design. Because the subconscious mind cannot distinguish between a real event and one that is vividly imagined, when it receives a picture of a goal as if it were already achieved, it interprets this as a fact and responds accordingly, removing any mental roadblocks in the process. In light of this understanding, the most effective way to expand your potential is to constantly expose your mind to a multisensory image of the end result you're striving for. These images serve as commands to the brain to reproduce outwardly what was created inwardly.

The two best times to practice visualization are right before you go to sleep and just after waking in the morning. Consider incorporating this into your First or Final Fifteen. If not every day, how about experimenting with once a week? Get relaxed and calm with the help of a few deep breaths. Then step into your own mental movie. See yourself doing what you would be doing if your prayer had been answered or your goal had already been accomplished. If you persist in holding the image of the life you believe God wants for you, that image is much more likely to become a fact.

Here's an action exercise for you: The next time you

pray about a particular problem, challenge, or issue currently facing you, take a few extra minutes to get really relaxed before you start praying. Take six or seven slow, deep breaths while imagining that your mind is completely free of old opinions, preconceived notions, your own knowledge, or entrenched negativity of any kind. Then ask God to fill your empty mind with his perfect wisdom. Affirm that you are open and receptive to direct inspiration from God—and mean it. Then visualize Jesus sitting next to you, coaching and advising you. Dwell upon the love, peace, and understanding in his eyes as you gladly receive his guidance. Finally, thank God for his perfect solution. Experience the surge of confidence you would have following such an encounter. This opportunity is ready when you are.

Strategy Six: Quarantine Negativity

Negativity spreads like the flu—not just from person to person, but also from one area of life to the next. Because of this, you may want to activate what I call Plan B. You can use this strategy if you find yourself unexpectedly dealing with a mess that won't disappear overnight. This is what you do if you cannot quickly prevent or eliminate negative circumstances. For example, maybe you are dealing with an ongoing financial problem or a difficulty with a child. Regardless of how you ended up in this bind, you need to take action to control any additional damage it could cause. Though it is important to use the other strategies mentioned in this book as a primary course of action, I want to share with you an underused yet extremely powerful method for limiting the damage negative situations and people can cause in your life. The method is this: *Schedule your negativity.*

I know what you are probably thinking. "It takes all the fun out of being negative when you have to schedule it. Unexpected negativity is the best kind, right?"

Hold on! Some other real benefits come from scheduling your negativity. First, when you take the spontaneity out of being negative, you drastically weaken the emotional energy it contains. You are better prepared to deal with it. If another person is involved, scheduling eliminates the ambush effect, which further reduces the unhealthy energy. When you schedule negativity, the problem often shrinks before your appointed time to deal with it arrives. The biggest benefit of "chunking" your negativity, though, is that you safeguard a much larger block of time that is then free of problems, difficulties, and other junk. Let's discuss two ways to use this technique.

First, if you are dealing with *chronic worry,* schedule a specific time each week to sit down and worry. Think of this as "worry on demand." Instead of scattering your problems and concerns over the entire week, group them into one specific time period. When a worry comes to mind during the week, capture it in writing and remind yourself that you have set aside Tuesday at 4 p.m. to deal with it. That should be enough to get it off your mind temporarily so that you can return to and enjoy other activities. Make a note of how many real worries still remain on Tuesday afternoon.

Second, in your marriage or your family life, you can schedule a weekly or daily *issue time* to deal with gripes, disappointments, and unmet expectations. Instead of giving everyone in the household free rein to spoil any given moment with a complaint, you target a specific time period and "do negativity" *by appointment only.* You will notice that this is very hard to do. You will also notice how a little progress goes a very long way. Many of my clients report being just "C" students with this quarantine strategy, yet they are still very pleased with the results. Put your own slant on this, and then give it a try.

Strategy Seven: Establish Ground Rules

Throughout this third section of the book, my objective has been to help you become more intentional with your inputs—the things you allow into your heart. Toward that end, I want to share five simple principles that you might want to remember as the Laws of Input:

1. **Environment.** You are heavily influenced by your physical surroundings, especially the things you read, watch, and listen to, as well as the words and images that consistently capture your attention. *Where* you are reinforces *who* you are.
2. **Association.** You will gradually take on the habits, attitudes, convictions, worldview, and sometimes even the body language and mannerisms of the people you habitually spend time with.
3. **Excluded Alternative.** When you say yes to the wrong inputs, you are by default saying no to the right inputs. When you *invest* time with the right people, you are protected from *spending* time with the wrong people.

4. Non-neutrality. All inputs contribute to who you become as a person! Nothing is neutral. Every exposure either overtly or discreetly influences your personality, your character, and the choices you make during the day, even though you are consciously unaware of most of them.

5. Attraction. Over time, you will draw into your life the conditions, events, people, and possibilities that correspond with your thinking. Your visible life on the outside is a mirror-image reflection of your invisible thought life, most of which has been shaped by your consistent inputs.

With these principles in mind, I want you to establish five ground rules for what you will allow into your heart. The rules you develop are up to you; my sole interest is in helping you become intentional in this vital area. In other words, I don't want you to wing it. Here are a few sample ground rules borrowed from my clients in The 1% Club:

- I invest most of my discretionary time with people of equal or greater character, and I reevaluate my progress in this area every ninety days.
- I listen to inspirational and educational audio programs in the car whenever I travel alone.
- I watch only television programs that are appropriate to watch with my kids.
- I plan my positive mental nutrition one week in advance.
- I read something wholesome and positive before

going to bed and immediately upon awakening in the morning.

In addition to the examples above, use the following questions to guide your first draft:

- Who do I want to become as a person, and what are my most important lifetime goals?
- Do I, or will I, desire my current exposures for my children? If not, what should I change?
- Which people in my life challenge me to high standards?
- Which people enable me to ease up on my priorities?
- How much *positive mental nutrition* do I want to consume each day or week?
- What do I listen to in the car most of the time?
- How much TV is the right amount for me, given my other goals?
- What kinds of programs should I increase, limit, or eliminate?
- How would I like to change because of what I read?
- If I don't make any changes in what I allow into my heart and mind, what kind of person will I be in ten years?

The point of putting together your ground rules is to help you decide *in advance* what you are going to fill your mind with on an ongoing basis. If you don't make that decision ahead of time, it is very easy to be swept along by cultural mores and conformed to what is current, trendy, and convenient, rather than being transformed by the renewing of your mind.

A Prayer for Protection

Lord God,

Thank you for all the positive influences in my life today. Thank you for everyone who has ever prayed for me and for anyone who will pray for me in the future. Thanks especially for the people of strong faith that you have placed in my path and the positive impact they have had on my character.

Insulate me from experiences that compromise my full potential. Keep me tuned in to the conforming power of my environment and consistent exposures. Move me away from distractions, diversions, and temptations. Keep my thoughts fixed instead on what is true, pure, excellent, and worthy of praise. I know that nothing guards my heart more than being in your will.

Protect me, Father, from any person or relationship that would slowly prod me down the wrong path. Cause me to become hypersensitive to the people in my life and the sometimes subtle influence they are having on my spiritual, emotional, mental, and physical habits. Bring wise, genuine friends into my life, and dissolve any ties with those who may weaken my relationship with you.

In Jesus' name,

Amen

This One Thing I Do . . .

Beginning today, I increase my potential for joy by personalizing and then memorizing one Bible verse that reminds me of how much God loves me and wants me to live with joy.

CHAPTER 9

THANKS FOR EVERYTHING

Living with Gratitude

The greatest thing is to give thanks for everything. He who has learned this knows what it means to live. He has penetrated the whole mystery of life: giving thanks for everything.

– Albert Schweitzer

My goal for this chapter is to help you become aware of the power of gratitude to help you live a strong, joy-filled life. You probably recognize that gratitude is vital to a life of joy. But are you expressing that appreciation today with your thoughts, words, and actions? Would your friends, family, and coworkers agree with you? Do you stand out as an exceptionally grateful person? Our hectic, often overloaded modern culture can easily distract us from following through on our good intentions. It is easier than ever to take our blessings for granted.

How grateful are you? Take a moment to evaluate yourself using these questions:

- What is positive and unique about your family?
- What are three of your best memories from your first year with your spouse?

- What is the most magnificent goal you have already accomplished?
- What parts of your body tend to work really well most of the time?
- In what ways has God shown his grace in your life recently?
- What is the nicest compliment you have received in the last month?
- What is the most valuable lesson you have learned from another person?
- What is the most beautiful thing you've seen in the last week?
- What is an old crisis or rough situation from the past that in retrospect has turned into a blessing or benefited you in some way?
- What is the number one thing you are going to be grateful for this time next year?

How did you do? Have you appropriately given thanks to God for the blessings that surround you? Do the people you love the most know how grateful you are for them?

Have you ever thought of intentionally cultivating the lost art of gratitude? It just might be the one indispensable ingredient in your recipe for a joy-filled life. Throughout the pages that follow, you are going to become tuned in to the transforming power of gratitude. I think you already know what to do—notice the blessings in your life, thank God for them, and express your gratitude to other people. With this chapter, I want you to start *doing more of what you already know!* You will find that your capacity for joy increases as your sense of gratitude grows. Whenever you feel thankful for a certain aspect of your life, or for your life in general, you are in sync with the 4:8 Principle. Remember from chapters 5 and 6 that you feel what you dwell upon. Far from being an accurate gauge of the quality of your life, your emotions reveal the quality of your thinking at any given moment.

When you experience a sense of gratitude, it means that you have been harboring thoughts of appreciation for the abundance in your life. When you feel a sense of deficiency, it does not necessarily mean that you are lacking something important. What it does mean is that you have recently been thinking about what is absent, very likely to the exclusion of what is *present*. You might have been thinking about your spouse's annoying quirks and overlooking all the reasons you married him in the first place. You might have been thinking about being under financial pressure and forgetting that you have just about everything money can't buy.

173

Gratitude is a conviction, a practice, and a discipline. It's an essential nutrient, a kind of spiritual amino acid for human growth, creativity, and joy. Gratitude involves channeling your energy and attention toward what is present and working rather than what's absent and ineffective. Gratitude is like a mental gearshift that takes you from turbulence to peacefulness, from stagnation to creativity. Gratitude brings you back to the present moment, to all that is working well in your life right now. **Gratitude is the cornerstone of an unstoppable attitude.** And gratitude can be cultivated and then experienced at ever-deepening levels.

Gratitude is also an effective antidote to most negative emotions. You cannot experience gratitude and hostility at the same time; you have to make a choice. Which one is it going to be? The more you appreciate today, the more things you will notice tomorrow to be grateful for. On the flip side, the less appreciative you are today, the fewer blessings you will tend to acknowledge tomorrow. The Greek philosopher Epictetus said, "He is a wise man who does not grieve for the things which he has not but rejoices for those which he has."

174

You are going to draw more joy out of your business, out of your marriage, out of your family life, and out of all the other aspects of your existence when you make a commitment to become a genuinely grateful person. The power of gratitude is undeniably immense.

Obstacles to Gratitude

If gratitude is so vital, why isn't everybody doing it? Because it is both a skill and a feeling. It is a choice and a reaction. Several common obstacles may water down your capability to appreciate your blessings to the fullest. Each of them can leave you feeling deficient. When you are alert to these gratitude obstacles, you can minimize their influence so they will not obstruct your potential for joy.

1. Excessive "noise." By this I am referring to the sheer velocity of life. The constant connection to commitments, obligations, and looming deadlines via mobile phones and e-mail keeps us preoccupied with urgency. Think about it: How often do you receive a call on your cell phone regarding one of your long-term goals? How often do you receive an e-mail that reminds you to appreciate your spouse or invest more time with your kids? Very rarely. Those tools of convenience and efficiency are designed to help you react quickly to the immediate demands of the day, not to take action on your most important values.

2. Overexposure to the media. Watching excessive television and "over-reading" the newspaper tends to remind us of what's not going well in the world. On the other hand, it provides plenty of material to pray about. Do you agree that the profusion of media sources seems to provide an avalanche of information but a clear deficit of wisdom? Watching the news exposes us to lots of problems but very few solutions. I don't know the answer, but how much news do we really need? It is worth pondering. This doesn't mean that to be grateful you've got to get rid of your TV or stop reading the newspaper, but you could cut back a little and see if it makes the positive difference for you that it has made for many of my clients. Try it and judge by the results. Often, when you decrease your intake of current events and other timely exposures and increase your ingestion of timeless materials, the result is a palpable difference in your outlook.

3. The "owe-me" attitude. This is the relatively modern notion that someone or some group owes us; that we deserve something from others. With this mentality, even if we receive something, it's not a gift but a right. This attitude dissolves gratitude on the spot. Nothing is quite so powerful, and so quickly destructive to your potential for joy, as the attitude of entitlement, or the "culture of complaint," as some have labeled it. Moaners and whiners surround us, and they often seem to be competing to see who has the worst grievance against society or who can be the most offended. Though we may laugh at this dynamic or try to distance ourselves from it, it is rubbing off on far too many people and infecting upcoming generations. Those who consume without contributing to society develop a deep sense of emptiness, which suspends the emotion of gratitude indefinitely.

Closely related to entitlement, but typically on a more interpersonal level, is what I call the Law of Familiarity. This simply means that the longer you've been exposed to a particular blessing in your life, the more likely you are to take it for granted. You begin to feel *entitled* to it rather than being *grateful* for it. To maximize your potential for joy, you must go out of your way to make sure you are not taking for granted the wonderful relationships and other blessings in your life. Remember, gratitude expands joy, and entitlement shrinks it.

> A proud man is seldom a grateful man, for he never thinks he gets as much as he deserves.
> – Henry Ward Beecher

4. Worry, or negative forecasting. This RAT is different from being concerned or conscientious, which is always accompanied by productive action. Worry involves dwelling on potential negative outcomes *without doing anything about them.* Worry is the result of dwelling on what you hope doesn't happen but fear *will* happen! If you were predicting positive outcomes, you would not be worrying, right? Worry is when you trust your fears more than you trust God. In the two verses immediately preceding Philippians 4:8, Paul writes, "Don't worry about anything; instead, pray about everything. Tell God what you need, and thank him for all he has done. Then you will experience God's peace, which exceeds anything we can understand. His peace will guard your hearts and minds as you live in Christ Jesus" (Philippians 4:6-7, NLT).

The worst part of worry is that it displaces and then dissolves genuine thoughts of gratitude. You cannot worry and be grateful at the same moment. You can waver, of course. You can worry for a few moments, be grateful for a few moments, worry for a few moments, and so on. Ever had a day like this? I know I have. But it doesn't have to be like this. When you deliberately concentrate on current blessings or even future blessings, worry fades away. It drops out of your life. Of course, this takes a little practice, but you will experience progress the first time you give it a try. It's been helpful for me to remember these words from Mark Twain: "I have been through some terrible things in my life, some of which actually happened." Most of what we worry about never come to pass. To relax the stronghold of chronic worry, review and put into action the quarantine strategy from the last chapter.

5. Materialism and consumerism. One humorous way to label this obstacle is *continuous deficiency syndrome* (CDS for short). This part curse, part blessing comes with the territory of being human. The benefits include technological breakthroughs and other societal advances. In a sense, our consumer society owes its very existence to its flair for fueling discontentment and an unquenchable appetite for more stuff. We are bombarded with thousands of marketing images every day reminding us that

177

- We could be richer.
- Our spouse could be even nicer.
- We could be thinner.
- Our breath could be fresher.
- Our whites could be whiter.
- Our carpets could be cleaner.
- Our children could be sharper, and so on.

CDS can dominate our attitudes unless we consciously counteract it with gratitude. The more that people seek to become satisfied as consumers, the emptier they can become as human beings. Gratitude, on the other hand, makes us feel that we have enough. Ingratitude leaves us in a state of deprivation in which we are constantly pursuing something else. Think about it. Where have you been looking for satisfaction recently? To material possessions? To intellectual distinction? To social standing? In light of your past experience, why do you think you will be happy with just a little bit more?

6. A scarcity mentality. This is an all-too-common belief that the pie of abundance contains only a fixed number of pieces. It's the deep-rooted fear that there is not enough of "the good stuff" for everyone. Of course, God's creation is not limited or scarce in the least, but when we mistakenly think it is, then for all practical purposes, it is—for us. A scarcity mind-set is characterized by thoughts such as *If she wins, then I lose* or *If he gets those, then I don't.* But consider that you can bake a bigger pie. You can create more value in your home, in your community, and in the world, and this abundance is self-perpetuating. The more you create, the more people are impacted and the more abundance is multiplied. You experience lasting abundance only when you realize that you already have everything you need for total joy.

7. Lack of a connection and intimacy with God. You see that I have saved the best for last. When you are right with God, you naturally and humbly cherish life for what it is—a temporary gift, a treasure with an unknown expiration date. This connection

Only the really thoughtful are truly grateful.

179

with God naturally breeds an awe of life as well as thankfulness for what life has to offer and what you are here to offer the world. As Jesus said, "I am the vine; you are the branches. If a man remains in me and I in him, he will bear much fruit; apart from me you can do nothing" (John 15:5, NIV).

The Nature of Gratitude

Now that you know the resistance you might face, I want to challenge you—for the rest of this book and beyond—to think of gratitude in three distinct ways. These ways will encourage you to actively practice gratitude and will cause your potential for joy to surge to an all-time high.

- **Gratitude is a *feeling*.** It is a sense of joy and appreciation in response to receiving a gift, whether that is a concrete object or an abstract gesture.
- **Gratitude is a *capacity*.** It is the learned skill of uncovering and creating meaning and value in everyday situations and relationships.

- **Gratitude is a *choice*.** It is a conscious and deliberate decision to focus on life's blessings rather than its shortcomings. Life will always have shortcomings, and it will always have virtues. When you focus on your blessings, your life feels abundant. When you focus on what's missing, life feels incomplete. As you know by now, where you point the spotlight is purely a matter of choice.

180

However you think of it, gratitude is a powerful magnetic force that naturally draws joy-filled people and occurrences into your life. I am glad to report that gratitude is not something you're born with. We can at least be thankful for that, right? Gratitude can be learned and cultivated throughout your lifetime. But is it possible to grow your gratitude to the point that it is visible to others?

> Assume the attitude,
> though you have it not.
> — William Shakespeare

Does Your Gratitude Stand Out?

Does your gratitude stand out above the crowd right now? Remember, by giving more gratitude, you get to keep more joy! What would have to happen for you to develop a reputation for being a highly grateful person? To become known for your gratitude, you first have to make the shift from *routine* to *exceptional* gratitude.

Routine gratitude is standard gratitude. It is ordinary, reactive, and often superficial. This includes saying thank you after receiving a gift or a helpful gesture. When someone lets you in as you're merging into traffic, you think to yourself, or wave, a thank-you to the other driver. When somebody holds a door for you, you say thank you. When you're handed your food in the drive-through window, you thank the server. These are all typical instances of routine gratitude.

Some people develop an immediate sense of gratefulness and relief when they hear about an accident or a tragedy in someone else's life. This rocks them out of their complacency, and they feel grateful for their own life and safety as a result. This is also routine gratitude. Wouldn't it be wonderful, though, if we didn't need other people's sorrows to remind us of the blessings in our own life? In today's world, it is easy to become desensitized to all but the most horrendous tragedies. We can overhear somebody talking about a horrible car crash or a crime that was committed, and it blows right over our heads. It just skims the surface; it hardly even bothers us. It even appears that the reactive yet intense gratitude for our freedom, our families, and our faith triggered by the events of September 11, 2001, has already been dulled by the passage of time, at least for those without loved ones directly involved. The good news is that you have the option of moving to a whole new level of appreciation and thanksgiving.

This next stage is called **exceptional gratitude.** This is intentional, proactive, and extraordinary. It is consistent with the 4:8 Principle, and it is without a doubt the exception to the rule of routine gratitude. Anyone can be appreciative of something obvious and observable, but it takes a joy-filled person to perceive the mustard seed of potential in a thorny situation or with a difficult individual. Expressing thanks for even the smallest things is where *exceptional gratitude* starts. There's no need to wait for the perfect opportunity. Express gratitude for progress now! **Exceptional gratitude refers to acts of thankfulness unprompted by someone else's tragedy, pain, or misfortune. Exceptional gratitude doesn't require something to be missing before it's appreciated.** This kind of gratitude is what Paul had in mind when he wrote to the Thessalonians, "Give thanks in all circumstances, for this is God's will for you in Christ Jesus" (1 Thessalonians 5:18, NIV).

Sadly, we often act as if we're going to live forever, and that today is merely a dress rehearsal. We think we can always show up, catch up, or make up tomorrow. We convince ourselves that we'll get another chance. Have you ever wondered if the victim of today's car crash remembered to tell her family how much she loved and appreciated them? Was she aware of how much they really appreciated her? Every morning, unsuspecting people all over the world walk out their front door never to return home, victims of accidents, heart attacks, violence, and other unpredictable instances of sudden death. When you practice exceptional gratitude, you enjoy the peace of knowing that you've said what needs to be said and that you've appreciated the most important people in your life.

Exceptional gratitude also means staying aware of universal blessings, the things that benefit everyone. It is experiencing the power of gratitude through those things that are common to us all:

- God's love
- Our body
- Our brain
- Sunshine and rain
- Forests and deserts
- Mountains and beaches
- Freedom in all forms
- Technology
- Relationships
- And many more . . .

Exceptional gratitude means expressing thankfulness for the little things in life that aren't so little, such as smiles, hugs, music, indoor plumbing, air-conditioning, clean water, science, education, seat belts, antibiotics, our immune system, and second chances, just to scratch the surface.

Exceptional gratitude also involves the habit of appreciating other people. When something appreciates, it increases in value, right? When people are sincerely appreciated, their own self-worth is elevated as well. If you want to increase the value of something in your life, take better care of it. If you want to increase the value of key relationships, treasure them. At this moment in time, perhaps your spouse could really benefit from some exceptional gratitude. Or possibly it is your child or even your parents who are starving for appreciation. Whoever it is, take better care of them. Honor them with more interest and attention. Dwell on what's great about them. View them through the lens of Philippians 4:8. There is always something that's great or could be great. And there is a special bonus when you appreciate others: It increases not only their value but yours as well.

Nothing has motivated me more as a coach than the sincere appreciation I have received from my clients in The 1% Club over the years. On more than one occasion, I have received a note, a phone call, or an e-mail at just the right time that inspired me to go another mile—to study more, write more, speak more, encourage more, and strive to be more than I would have been or done otherwise.

> To be grateful is to recognize the love of God in everything he has given us and he has given us everything. Every breath we draw is a gift of his love. Every moment of existence is a grace for it brings with it immense graces from him. Gratitude therefore takes nothing for granted, is never unresponsive, is constantly awakening to new wonder and to praise of the goodness of God for the grateful person knows that God is good not by hearsay but by experience and that is what makes all the difference.
> — Thomas Meston

Forty Ways to Express Your Gratitude Now!

Are you ready to go on a thanksgiving binge? No, I am not referring to a holiday stuffing. I am talking about building rapid momentum toward an exceptionally grateful lifestyle, a way of living that automatically aligns your thoughts with the 4:8 Principle and protects your heart from the forces of negativity. The thought stimulators below supply you with a quick-start game plan for upgrading your gratitude. Most of these ideas have been shared with me by my clients. Now they are yours! I encourage you to claim the ideas as your own and start implementing those that strike a chord with you. The binge officially begins now.

1. At night, count your blessings silently as you drift off to sleep.
2. Count your blessings as you lie in bed in the morning after the alarm clock goes off.
3. Journal your blessings for three minutes immediately after waking up in the morning.
4. Make a list of what you expect to be thankful for ten years from now.
5. Before grace at mealtime, discuss specific things you are grateful for as a family.
6. Every day send a brief thank-you e-mail to someone who's been helpful in any way, large or small.
7. Leave mini thank-you notes around the house to let your family know you notice their efforts.
8. Leave quick thank-you notes around the office to ensure that coworkers know you notice their efforts.
9. Make a list of twenty-one things you are grateful for, and meditate on that list for fifteen minutes without distraction.

10. Journal your blessings for three minutes before getting into bed at night.

11. Go the extra mile to help someone who has helped you.

12. Go the extra mile to help someone who has not helped you.

13. Ask God for a greater sense of awe and appreciation.

14. Create fun surprises or little rewards for those you appreciate.

15. Ask the important people in your life what makes them feel appreciated.

16. Repeat the affirmation "I am so blessed. I am so blessed." Repeat this silently over and over again as you fall asleep, as you exercise, or as you drive somewhere by yourself.

17. Thank someone belatedly for the help, encouragement, or assistance they provided in the past.

18. Give yourself a special treat to express appreciation that you are unique and irreplaceable.

19. Show gratitude for a particular loved one as if it were your last opportunity to do so.

20. Itemize all the possessions in one room of your house. Thank God for those you're glad to have, and then give or throw the rest away.

21. Make a list of seven people who have taught you important life lessons.

22. Praise God for the aspects of your life that are working really well right now.

23. Make a list of mistakes that you are fortunate not to have made.
24. Tell God how grateful you are for every time you have been awarded a second chance at something.
25. Recall the best choices you've made as an adult.
26. Discuss with a good friend some of the things you used to want but now you are glad you don't have.
27. Send a handwritten thank-you note to someone every week.
28. Sit perfectly still, with no distractions or noise, for fifteen minutes.
29. Carve out a little time each week to review the positive things that happened in the previous week.
30. Write a brief note of encouragement to someone who would never expect it from you.
31. Greet everyone with the type of smile you'd exhibit if you had just received great news.
32. Maintain a log of goals accomplished or prayers answered.
33. Review with your spouse or a close friend all the positive things that happened the previous month.
34. Offer prayers of thanksgiving in advance for the exciting things you believe God is going to do in your life.
35. Write a previous teacher, coach, professor, or employer, thanking them for what you appreciate about them.
36. Write a formal letter of thanks to a significant positive influence in your life today.

37. Show extreme gratitude for your own physical body by upgrading the way you treat it for a designated seventy-two-hour period.
38. Say a quick prayer of thanks for all the things in your life that don't need fixing.
39. Make a list of all the people who have pushed you to become a better person.
40. Pray for extra blessings in the life of someone who did not believe in you and as a result motivated you to prove yourself.

Now you should have plenty of ideas! In fact, I suspect you have far more than you could possibly use. You can't say your coach didn't try, can you? But, I am curious. Which idea spoke to you the most? Which idea are you going to put into practice first? What idea could you use *today*? And who besides yourself will be blessed as a result of your effort?

Do you remember that my goal for this chapter was to help you become hypersensitive to the power of gratitude in living a joy-filled life? Did I reach my goal? I think that depends on what steps you take next.

To wrap up this final chapter, I'd like to thank you for demanding a higher standard. Thank you for pushing the envelope of your full potential. Thank you for seeking a joy-filled life! Thank you for reading *The 4:8 Principle*. And thank you for sharing this book and these ideas with those you love and care about the most. Thanks for everything!

A Prayer of Appreciation

Dear Lord,

Thank you for all that you are. I praise you for your unlimited power. You are ready and willing to help me with anything. I praise you for your boundless love. I know you are committed to what's best for me.

I praise you, Lord, for knowing everything. Thank you for having answers to all my questions and solutions to all my problems. I praise you for being the source of all goodness in my life. Thank you for supplying my every need in abundance.

189

I praise you for being my ever-present Good Shepherd. Thank you for being a real, vivid, and active power in my life—today, always, and forevermore. Mostly, though, thank you for your grace and mercy, my ultimate source of joy.

In Jesus' name,

Amen

This One Thing I Do . . .

Beginning today, I increase my potential for joy by thanking God in advance for all the wonderful blessings he has in store for me over the next ten years.

PART THREE SUMMARY

Defending Your Joy

- We often allow negative ideas and others' opinions to corrupt our potential for joy. If you take the initiative, you can construct your own firewall and insulate your mental software from these joy bandits.

- Authentic joy can always be identified by the unmistakable leap of faith that comes first. To activate this faith, align your attitude with your prayers even before you have a concrete reason to be hopeful.

- Hanging around people who have no real vision or who limit God with their own caustic attitudes puts you at serious risk of slipping to their level. Even worse, you likely will not notice that your character is changing. Actively seek good company and positive influences.

- Gratitude is a conviction, a practice, and a discipline. It's a spiritual nutrient for human growth, creativity, and joy. Gratitude can be cultivated and then experienced at progressively deeper levels.

Guard Your Heart

The 4:8 Challenge

1. How intentional are you in the way you use the First Fifteen and Final Fifteen minutes of the day?

What typically captures your attention immediately before falling asleep at night?

2. How could you better use your time in the car to learn, grow, and stay focused on what is lovely, pure, excellent, and worthy of praise?

3. Are your associations in sync with your ambitions? Are you now investing enough time with people who build your character? If not, how can you get back on track?

4. In what ways could you express appreciation to your loved ones in the next twenty-four hours? How could you maintain this habit indefinitely?

191

YOU ARE WHAT YOU THINK!

May we shout for joy when we hear of your victory
  and raise a victory banner in the name of our God.
May the LORD answer all your prayers.
Psalm 20:5 (NLT)

Well done!

Now that you've reached the end of *The 4:8 Principle,* I want to give you an action plan and some additional tools to make it even easier for you to put the principles you've been learning into practice—sooner rather than later. Most important, you will find some extra resources in this Afterword to help you sustain your progress.

The first step to better thinking and a joy-filled existence here on earth is to become aware of your thought life. Most people are simply swept up in the turbulent current of reactive thoughts, feelings, and behaviors. Essentially unaware of the connection between their state of mind and their circumstances, they passively live out a frustratingly repetitive life script that eventually causes them to settle for far less than their God-given best. This is *not* for you—especially now that you've learned the 4:8 Principle!

Whatever your life is like right now, you can get to the next level if you truly think you can. Your potential for joy is limited only by your level of commitment to think joyful thoughts most of the time. But before you'll see improvement, you must change your thinking. Any other type of change will be only temporary.

In a very real sense, you are what you think you are. Start, then, by changing your thought life. Renew your mind! Fortunately, it can be quite simple when you organize your efforts around the 4:8 Principle.

In the Introduction, I mentioned that I wrote *The 4:8 Principle* to propel you into new ways of thinking, speaking, and acting. Now that you've read the book, in what ways are you already looking at your world a little differently? In what ways are you filtering your circumstances through the 4:8 Principle? As your coach, allow me to challenge you to take just a moment to evaluate your grasp of the 4:8 Principle with the quick review that follows. After reading the questions for each chapter, rate your understanding on a scale of 1–10 (with 10 being the highest level). You'll find these summary questions great for a small-group study as well.

PART ONE

Think on These Things
Discovering Your Joy

___ CHAPTER 1 | Life as It Was Meant to Be: *Discovering the Secret to a Joy-Filled Life*

What is the secret to a joy filled life? In what ways do many people search for joy in all the wrong places? Why is it important to demonstrate joy in the way we run our lives? Why do you choose the thoughts that you think? Up to this point, have you been a faithful steward of your mental life? How so, exactly?

___ CHAPTER 2 | A New Beginning: *Focusing on What Produces Joy*

Why is it so common to tell ourselves destructive things? What would you have to give up to start thinking more consistently in accordance with Philippians 4:8? Can you name some improvements in your life that do not first involve changed thinking? How is it possible to see opportunities where there were previously only problems? How could you use 4:8 Questions to discipline your mind?

___ CHAPTER 3 | Wow, That's Me!: *Embracing Your God-Given Identity*

How does your self-concept influence your potential for joy? Where does a mediocre self-concept come from? What is your self-ideal, and how is it relevant to the 4:8 Principle? In what ways could you override past negative programming?

As of today, who is the "Imposter" in your life? How could thinking like a world-class athlete help you better practice the 4:8 Principle? Have you given yourself permission to live life to the fullest?

PART TWO

Power, Love, and a Sound Mind
Developing Your Joy

____ CHAPTER 4 | Your Potential for Joy: *Fortifying Your Self-Concept*

What is the true source of self-worth? How can seeking approval from others interfere with your potential for joy? How does your self-concept improve when you "agree with your Creator"? What's the payback for hanging on to old wounds and feeding them with attention? How does guilt shrink your potential for joy? In light of God's best plans for your life, what kind of private conversations should you be having with yourself on a daily basis? Do you agree that joy is much like "proactive happiness"?

____ CHAPTER 5 | You Make Me So Mad!: *Taking Charge of Your Emotional Life*

Are you maximizing each moment with the interest, wonder, and excitement of a young child? Do you affirm God more often than you affirm your adversity? What are your emotional goals and what must you do differently to experience those desired feelings more frequently? Are you still hanging on to thoughts that haven't helped you very much in the past? How can you use the Law of Exchange to rapidly strengthen your emotional life? When you "don't feel like it," is it dishonest or fake to behave in a manner consistent with your values . . . or is it just an act of discipline? How are negative emotions similar to a pot of boiling water?

___ CHAPTER 6 | Head Games: *Starving Negative Emotions*

How does choosing 4:8 Thoughts help to manufacture the emotional life you want? What is the connection between your emotional strength and your moral decisions? What are some of the RATs (really awful thoughts) that have pestered your emotional life up until now? How does accepting responsibility defuse negative emotions? How can "venting" both help and hurt an important relationship? How can practicing compassion toward others actually improve your own emotional health? Stress and tension are most likely signs of what process?

PART THREE

Guard Your Heart
Defending Your Joy

___ CHAPTER 7 | Your Personal Firewall: *Developing Habits to Protect Your Heart*

How do the things you read, watch, and listen to influence your potential for joy? In what ways are your current circumstances like a mirror of your mental and emotional life? In what ways are you the gatekeeper of your mind? Why should you watch television only in moderation? Do the first fifteen minutes of your morning glorify God and set the foundation for a joy-filled day? Why is bedtime quite possibly the worst time to be negative?

_____ CHAPTER 8 | Junk-Proof Your Mind: *Strategies for a Healthy Mind*

How much joy do you think you can stand? Do most of the people you spend time with amplify your joy? How does memorizing Bible verses activate the Law of Exchange? Do you generally talk more about the things you want in life or the things you hope to avoid? How often do you envision the awesome future that God has planned for you? What would happen if you started scheduling your negativity (complaining, worrying, etc.)? To maximize your potential for joy, what ground rules should you establish for junk-proofing your mind?

_____ CHAPTER 9 | Thanks for Everything: *Living with Gratitude*

Have you appropriately given thanks to God for the blessings that surround you? Do the people you love the most know how grateful you are for them? What gratitude blockages weigh you down the most? In what ways does your gratitude stand out? What is the difference between routine and exceptional gratitude? How are you consistently appreciating the most important people in your life?

RECAP

How did you do? Did you identify some areas where your thinking is already lined up with Philippians 4:8? Did you discover a blind spot or an area of weakness? In the spirit of the 4:8 Principle, I want you to consider any weak spot as an area of opportunity, not as a problem or limitation. Think back to chapter 2, A New Beginning. Consider the questions we raised and the key question you must now answer:

Would you like to grow in your faith?   **199**
> *What change in your thinking must come first?*

Would you like to overcome a particular heartache?
> *What change in your thinking must come first?*

Would you like to break out of a tiresome rut?
> *What change in your thinking must come first?*

Do you want to get closer to your spouse?
> *What change in your thinking must come first?*

Would you like to develop a Christlike character?
> *What change in your thinking must come first?*

Would you like to have even greater influence in the lives of your children?
> *What change in your thinking must come first?*

Do you aspire to higher levels of physical energy and vitality?
> *What change in your thinking must come first?*

Would you like to be more emotionally resilient?
> *What change in your thinking must come first?*

Would you like to be in a stronger position financially?
What change in your thinking must come first?

Would you like to overcome a specific self-defeating habit?
What change in your thinking must come first?

Would you like to make a bigger difference in your business or community?
What change in your thinking must come first?

Would you like to be joy filled?
What change in your thinking must come first?

THE ANSWER IS THE QUESTION

We all want to experience a fuller, deeper, more meaningful life. Who wouldn't want to be joy filled? But how do we actually reach that goal? It starts with a change of thinking. When you change the questions you consistently ask yourself, you start thinking differently. When you ask better questions, you receive better answers.

In the upcoming section, you will find a variety of sample 4:8 Questions to help keep your mind joy filled. For even greater benefit, I encourage you to also draft your own questions in the spaces provided underneath each category.

Sample Morning 4:8 Questions

(Ask these questions immediately upon waking up.)

1. What am I grateful to God for this morning?
2. What are my strengths, and how can I use them today?

3. What are three of my recent victories, and who was blessed as a result?
4. What relationships could I affect positively today?
5. What am I excited about experiencing over the next twelve hours?

Craft Your Own Morning 4:8 Questions

1. _____

2. _____

3. _____

4. _____

5. _____

Sample Evening 4:8 Questions

(Ask these questions before falling asleep at night.)

1. What worked well for me today?
2. What's great about my family life?
3. Who could I encourage or appreciate tomorrow?
4. What choices tomorrow will increase my energy?
5. In what ways could I increase my service in the next twenty-four hours?

Craft Your Own Evening 4:8 Questions

1. _____

2. _____

3. _____

4. _____

5. _____

Sample Daily Questions for a 4:8 Marriage

(Ask these questions early and often.)

1. What's great about my marriage right now?
2. What could I do in the next forty-eight hours to make it even stronger?
3. What do I really love about my spouse, and how could I express my appreciation today?
4. What are the best things we could do together and get really excited about in the next ninety days?
5. In what ways could I take better care of myself this week and as a result take better care of my spouse?

Craft Your Own Questions for a 4:8 Marriage

1. _____

2. _____

3. _____

4. _____

5. _____

Sample Daily Questions for 4:8 Parents

(Ask these questions to renew your parenting spirit.)

1. What's awesome about being a parent?

2. What are five of my virtues as a parent?

3. What strength could I nurture in my child today?

4. What *coachable* moments could I create today?

5. What am I looking forward to as a parent in the next month?

Craft Your Own Daily Questions for 4:8 Parents

1. _____

2. _____

3. _____

4. _____

5. _____

Sample Daily Questions for 4:8 Kids

(These questions are awesome before bedtime.)

1. What things am I thankful for, and how could I show my gratitude?

2. What progress did I make today? (achievements, improvements, discoveries, compliments, and other neat stuff)

3. What am I looking forward to and excited about in the next week?

4. What am I really good at, or what could I be great at if I practiced more often?

5. What's a fun goal or cool idea I'd like to work on tomorrow?

Craft Your Own Daily Questions for 4:8 Kids

1. _____

2. _____

3. _____

4. _____

5. _____

Sample Daily Questions for Facing Adversity

(Ask these questions as needed.)

1. What blessings surround me today?
2. What's great about this situation, or what could be great?
3. How might this situation be a blessing in disguise?
4. What lessons could I be learning?
5. What productive steps could I take today?

Craft Your Own Daily Questions for Facing Adversity

1. _____

2. _____

3. _____

4. _____

5. _____

JOY-PROMOTING THOUGHTS

An affirmation is a perfect expression of faith. By affirming what we hope for and pray for, we strengthen the belief that its attainment is forthcoming. Affirmations help train our minds to spot the blessings that God has already poured into our lives. They are a highly effective faith-building tool. The following pages contain examples of these joyful thoughts in a variety of categories. Think of each affirmation as a positive mental vitamin or "thought conditioner." For added value, develop your own affirmations in the spaces provided.

Affirm Maximum Energy

- I desire maximum energy!

- I dissolve negative emotions!

- I crave lean protein, healthy carbs, and essential fats.

- I think and speak of myself only as healthy and vibrant.

- I drink lots of pure water.

- I balance stress with recovery.

- I plan my meals and snacks.

- My metabolism works effectively.

- I am free of destructive lifestyle habits.

- I take time to be still with God daily.

- I am immune to bad news, gossip, and other negativity.

- I am turbocharged and ready to positively affect others!

Compose Your Own Thoughts Affirming Maximum Energy

- _____
- _____
- _____
- _____

- _____

Affirm Unshakable Faith

- My faith is beyond strong!

- I love God and trust him completely.

- I am bold!

- I joyfully receive unshakable faith.

- I schedule time daily to be with God.

- I surround myself with people of strong faith.

- I am transformed by the renewing of my mind.

- I memorize Scripture.

- I let go and let God . . .

- I believe in God's goodness.

- I think about what is lovely, gracious, and excellent.

- My lifestyle supports my unshakable faith.

AFTERWORD: YOU ARE WHAT YOU THINK!

Compose Your Own Thoughts Affirming Unshakable Faith

- _____

- _____

- _____

- _____

- _____

Affirm High Performance

- I am responsible.

- I take action every day to accomplish my goals.

- I am a learning machine!

- I am confident and bold!

- I am patient and persistent.

- I surround myself with winners.

- With God's help, I get it done.

- I give with passion!

- I am a well-adjusted, balanced, and extremely capable human being.

- I have impeccable honesty.

- I have written specific and challenging life goals.

- I rewrite and review my goals daily.

Compose Your Own Thoughts Affirming High Performance

- _____
- _____
- _____
- _____
- _____

Affirm Marriage

- I put God at the center of my marriage.

- I bathe my relationship in prayer.

- I easily forgive myself and my spouse.

- I communicate clearly and specifically.

- I am patient, kind, and reasonable.

- I look for and see the strengths in my mate.

- I take the initiative to keep our marriage strong.

- I am relaxed, self-confident, and fun.

- I amplify joy in our marriage!

- I exercise and stay energetic.

- I am financially responsible.

- I cherish my spouse with my daily choices.

Compose Your Own Thoughts Affirming Marriage

- _____
- _____
- _____
- _____
- _____   **209**

Affirm Effective Parenting

- I am a responsible parent.
- I am clear about my priorities.
- I know the goal of my parenting.
- I set a godly example with my life.
- I consistently encourage my children.
- My daily choices teach positive lessons.
- I establish clear boundaries and stand firm.
- I learn everything I can.
- I invest quantity time with my kids.
- I pray with and for my children.
- God is working through me and my family.
- I am raising high-character kids.

Compose Your Own Thoughts Affirming Effective Parenting

- _____

- _____

- _____

- _____

- _____

Affirm Peace of Mind

- I keep my thoughts on peace.

- I am calm and composed.

- I meditate on Scripture.

- I let stress melt away.

- I rely on God's strength.

- I take time to be still.

- My mind is tranquil and serene.

- I joyfully trust God.

- I choose peace.

- I am free of negativity.

- I experience comfort.

- God is with me always.

AFTERWORD: YOU ARE WHAT YOU THINK!

Compose Your Own Thoughts Affirming Peace of Mind

- _____
- _____
- _____
- _____
- _____

Affirm Your Children

- You are a beautiful, wonderful child of God.
- You love God more than anything else in the whole world.
- Mom and Dad love you forever, always, no matter what.
- You respect and obey Mom and Dad.
- With Christ, you are unstoppable!
- You make wise choices.
- You think for yourself.
- You choose your thoughts.
- You have goals.
- You smile a lot.
- You speak kind words to yourself and others.
- You are a one-of-a-kind masterpiece from God!

Compose Your Own Thoughts Affirming Your Children

- _____
- _____
- _____
- _____

- _____

Affirm Resourceful Responses to Adversity

- God is with me, helping me.
- I know that this, too, shall pass.
- I am learning what I need to learn.
- I trust God, no matter what.
- I keep my thoughts on God.
- I am filled with the peace of God.
- I do what I need to do.
- I ask for help.
- I take constructive action now.
- My faith is growing.
- I glorify God with my responses.
- I am seeing solutions.

AFTERWORD: YOU ARE WHAT YOU THINK!

Compose Your Own Thoughts Affirming Resourceful
Responses to Adversity

- _____

- _____

- _____

- _____

- _____

Affirm Financial Success

- I am a faithful steward.

- God is my source and provider.

- I utilize wise counsel.

- I focus on service and contribution.

- I pay bills with joy.

- I am comfortable with financial success.

- I believe in abundance.

- I let go of all stress concerning money.

- I have specific financial goals.

- I build financial margin.

- I tithe and give to worthy causes.

- I have plenty.

Compose Your Own Thoughts Affirming Financial Success

- _____

- _____

- _____

- _____

- _____

MEMORIZATION

As we discussed in chapter 8, memorizing Scripture is one of the simplest and surest methods for refreshing your mind. By committing Scripture verses to memory, you begin the process of forcing out negative, limiting thoughts and replacing them with the marvelous power and potential of God's promises. Remember, the Word of God does not lie dormant once internalized:

> For the word of God is alive and powerful. It is sharper than the sharpest two-edged sword, cutting between soul and spirit, between joint and marrow. It exposes our innermost thoughts and desires. (Hebrews 4:12, NLT)

You will find the verses below to be especially worthy of memorization. As you explore the Bible, you will find an unlimited supply of these spiritual gems. As you store these inspirational truths in your memory banks, you will be thrilled with the joy and strength you receive as a result. I recommend that you write one verse each week on a three-by-five card and carry it with you for the entire week, rereading it ten or twenty times a day.

1. PSALM 28:7 (ESV)

> *The LORD is my strength and my shield; in him my heart trusts, and I am helped; my heart exults, and with my song I give thanks to him.*

2. MATTHEW 11:28 (NIV)

> *Come to me, all you who are weary and burdened, and I will give you rest.*

3. NEHEMIAH 8:10 (NIV)

> *Do not grieve, for the joy of the LORD is your strength.*

4. PROVERBS 3:5 (NIV)

> *Trust in the LORD with all your heart and lean not on your own understanding.*

5. PHILIPPIANS 4:13 (NKJV)

> *I can do all things through Christ who strengthens me.*

6. ISAIAH 26:3 (NKJV)

> *You will keep him in perfect peace, whose mind is stayed on You, because he trusts in You.*

7. ROMANS 8:37 (NIV)

> *In all these things we are more than conquerors through him who loved us.*

8. GALATIANS 6:9 (NIV)

> *Let us not become weary in doing good, for at the proper time we will reap a harvest if we do not give up.*

9. JAMES 1:17 (NIV)

> *Every good and perfect gift is from above, coming down from the Father of the heavenly lights, who does not change like shifting shadows.*

10. PHILIPPIANS 2:5 (NKJV)

> *Let this mind be in you which was also in Christ Jesus.*

11. ISAIAH 30:15 (NLT)

> *In quietness and confidence is your strength.*

12. PSALM 91 (NIV)

> *He who dwells in the shelter of the Most High*
> *will rest in the shadow of the Almighty.*
> *I will say of the LORD, "He is my refuge and my fortress,*
> *my God, in whom I trust."*
> *Surely he will save you from the fowler's snare*
> *and from the deadly pestilence.*
> *He will cover you with his feathers,*
> *and under his wings you will find refuge;*
> *his faithfulness will be your shield and rampart.*
> *You will not fear the terror of night,*
> *nor the arrow that flies by day,*
> *nor the pestilence that stalks in the darkness,*
> *nor the plague that destroys at midday.*

A thousand may fall at your side,
*   ten thousand at your right hand,*
*   but it will not come near you.*
You will only observe with your eyes
*   and see the punishment of the wicked.*
If you make the Most High your dwelling—
*   even the LORD, who is my refuge—*
then no harm will befall you,
*   no disaster will come near your tent.*
For he will command his angels concerning you
*   to guard you in all your ways;*
they will lift you up in their hands,
so that you will not strike your foot against a stone.
You will tread upon the lion and the cobra;
*   you will trample the great lion and the serpent.*
"Because he loves me," says the LORD, "I will rescue him;
*   I will protect him, for he acknowledges my name.*
He will call upon me, and I will answer him;
*   I will be with him in trouble,*
*   I will deliver him and honor him.*
With long life will I satisfy him
*   and show him my salvation."*

My prayer is that *The 4:8 Principle* has "stirred up the gifts of God that are within you," and that you experience and spread God's joy throughout your life for the rest of your life!

INDIANA FARM
BUREAU INSURANCE®

1-10-12   11:39pm

ABOUT THE AUTHOR

Tommy Newberry is the founder and head coach of The 1% Club, an organization dedicated to helping entrepreneurs and their families maximize their full potential. As a pioneer in the life-coaching field since 1991, Tommy has equipped business leaders in more than thirty industries to work less, earn more, and enjoy greater satisfaction with the right accomplishments.

Tommy is the author of *Success Is Not an Accident; 366 Days of Wisdom & Inspiration;* and numerous audio programs, including the best-selling series Success Is Not an Accident: Secrets of the Top 1%. Known for his blunt, highly practical, and no-nonsense coaching style, Tommy has earned the title of America's Success Coach. His passion for developing the whole person is clearly evident throughout his live workshops, keynote presentations, books, and audio courses. Tommy's annual Couples Planning Retreat takes world-class planning tools into the family realm, allowing husbands and wives to design a more balanced, simplified, and enriching life together.

An avid goal setter, Tommy has earned certification as an emergency medical technician and PADI rescue diver, as well as holding a black belt in the Korean martial art of choi kwang do. He lives in Atlanta with his wife, Kristin, and their three boys. To contact Tommy, please visit www.tommynewberry.com.

Who's Coaching You?

Your success strategy doesn't end with a single book. Continue on your path toward personal excellence and lifelong fulfillment with The 1% Club's *Virtual Coach* program.

No travel. No workshops to attend. No schedule conflicts!

The *Virtual Coach* program keeps you playing your "A" game in each area of life. Regardless of where you live or work, you can tap into the ongoing power of The 1% Club with a minimum investment and on your own time schedule. Anytime, anywhere, you can learn, plan, practice, and implement these life-changing concepts—at your own pace and when it's convenient for you. Best of all, we'll stick with you over the long haul, pushing and challenging you to break through previous plateaus. If you can't be with us in person, this is the next best thing.

No more going it alone with this timeless system! We'll stick with you from start to finish. From weekly reminders and monthly performance advice to quarterly conference calls, we'll support you, step-by-step, toward your best year ever—and far beyond. Our mission is simple: to help you maximize your God-given potential in all areas of life. We've helped thousands already . . . *why not let us help you help yourself?* Anchored in the core principles of *Success Is Not an Accident*, the *Virtual Coach* equips you to

1. Clarify your most significant goals
2. Organize your life in alignment with your top values
3. Consistently nurture your most important relationships
4. Define your goals in such a way that you will naturally accelerate your progress
5. Stay on track, focused, and free of distractions
6. Overcome procrastination and other potential-limiting behaviors
7. Maximize physical, mental, and emotional energy
8. Reduce stress, tension, and worry
9. Refine your unique strengths
10. Build unstoppable self-confidence for the right risks
11. Eliminate clutter and other junk that bogs you down
12. Upgrade your earning, investing, and giving.

With this advanced coaching system, Tommy Newberry helps you build instant momentum and equips you to take command of yourself and your future—starting immediately. As a special thanks to readers of this book, enroll for a limited time with promo code "VCSUCCESS" and save $100 on registration. Learn more at www.1percentclub.com/virtualcoach, or call 1.888.663.7372, toll-free.

The 1% Club's
SuperFOCUS Program

Join other like-minded individuals in The 1% Club's SuperFOCUS Program. In just a half day every quarter, you'll evaluate your progress, share breakthrough ideas, and build unstoppable momentum toward your biggest goals. This one-of-a-kind coaching program keeps your entire life on purpose, energized, and organized around the few things that matter most.

BEYOND JUST LEARNING!

This is not a seminar, a lecture, or a one time event. Though you are certain to learn a lot during and between the quarterly workshops, this program is not about what you learn; it is about what you do differently. The SuperFOCUS is a one-of-a-kind group coaching experience that helps you strategically assess your present circumstances so that you will operate more effectively and consistently in the future.

WE STICK WITH YOU . . . YOU FOLLOW THROUGH!

Unlike one-day or weekend events, The 1% Club emphasizes follow-through and sustained positive change. As pioneers in the life-coaching field, we know that peak performance is not created from a motivational rally or from an inspirational class alone, but from ongoing exposure to

- the right people
- the right ideas
- the right tools, and
- the right encouragement.

The cumulative effect of repeated reinforcement, constructive feedback, and authentic accountability produces long-lasting results. You will also benefit from our experience in more than thirty diverse industries. We combine, filter, and share with you the best insights and strategies from other members of The 1% Club, so you gain a decisive advantage. From these true-life success stories, you will learn what really works in the field. For more information, please visit www.1percentclub.com/superfocus.

CP0116